COMPETING TO WIN

Lessons Learned for Reaching the Next Level of Organizational Performance

The Wisdom Chronicles

I0031632

first edition

Dr. Ted Marra

Published by:
Technics Publications, LLC
2 Lindsley Road
Basking Ridge, NJ 07920 USA
http://www.TechnicsPub.com

Technics

Publications

Cover design by Mark Brye
Edited by Erin Elizabeth Long

Copyright © 2014 by Dr. Ted Marra

ISBN, print ed. 9781634620062

First Printing 2015

Library of Congress Control Number: 2014957729

This book could not have been created without the guiding hand of my dear friend and colleague Philip Sadler. Our frequent discussions and his valuable input were always stimulating and carried me higher in my thinking. Then too I must thank another close friend and colleague, Dr. Lothar Natau, as much for his spiritual support as his tangible input to the process.

Table of Contents

Foreword

Ted Marra and I have had many conversations over a number of years. On these occasions we have talked about matters of common interest and shared our views on a wide range of topics. One recurring theme has been why some companies are able to sustain outstanding performance over many years while others are either marginally competitive or fail altogether. In chewing this over we have shared our knowledge based on what we have learned in the course of our work in different fields – in Ted's case as a global consultant working at the highest level in major international firms and in mine as CEO of an international business school and as a company director.

We agreed that there is no simple answer to this question – no magic bullet that is the key to success. Not surprising, since organizations are extremely complex systems. Achieving sustained business success depends on a range of factors, some hard and some soft. A CEO is like a conjuror who has to keep many balls in the air at the same time – if he takes his eye off one then the whole system can collapse. A global business operating in today's world has many more *balls in the air* than a juggling act. We also agreed that these balls are of two kinds. The first set are to do with leadership and the creation of a winning culture, about articulating a clear purpose for the organization – one going beyond shareholder value, developing a vision for the future and embedding a set of enduring values. The second are to do with the essentials of good management – strategic planning, measurement and control and, above all, execution. Tying all these factors together is the business model.

What Ted Marra has done in this remarkably compact volume is to provide today's and tomorrow's business leaders with an amazingly clear guide to achieving sustainable success, dealing with all these factors in turn and tying them together. He gives the reader some pertinent examples both from his own consulting experience and from his extensive knowledge of the managerial literature.

I derived particular value from the challenging questions he addresses to his readers at the end of each chapter. These are not simply adjuncts to the test, to be read and consigned to the bookshelf. They raise questions that each CEO, indeed each member of the top team needs to ask him or herself at regular intervals.

I strongly recommend this book to current and aspiring CEOs. It can be read in the course of a moderately long business flight. A productive use of time.

Philip Sadler CBE FCIPD FRSA
Vice-president and former CEO Ashridge Business School

Introduction
Outperforming the Rest

As the author of this work I will share a wealth of experience and opportunities for learning gained during some 40 years of practice with over 155 organizations of every description. I have seen organizations from many different industries, seen them succeed and fail, and seen them from a range of perspectives. I have held a variety of positions as CEO, Research Director, Vice President, consultant, business school professor, strategic facilitator, and organizational mentor.

I have worked in a diverse array of industries and sectors including banking, energy, tires, appliances, financial services, charities, central government, education, police, engineering, healthcare, vehicle manufacturing, and more.

What is it that truly makes the difference? Why, over the medium to long term do some organizations consistently outperform their peers? There is no one simple answer, no magic bullet. Human organizations are highly complex organisms and organizational behavior is influenced by many factors. **But what has been learned from my experience is that success comes down to getting a small number of critical things right.** Each chapter of this book looks at one of these critical factors.

Throughout this book the lessons learned of the past, identifying why some companies have gone from modest beginnings to global dominance of their markets and why other companies, once world leaders, have failed, will be highlighted.

At the same time you will be able to see the changing context of world business and why the key ongoing changes have meant that what was successful in the past will simply not ensure future success. To be successful in the third and fourth decades of the 21st century will require radical rethinking of the road to success.

> *If you want to escape the gravitational pull of the past, you have to be willing to challenge your own orthodoxy's, to regenerate your core strategies and rethink your most fundamental assumptions about how you are going to compete.*
>
> C. K. Pralahad

In sharing what I have learned with the reader, I hope that it will not only stretch your thinking, challenge your preconceptions and shift your paradigms, but change the way you manage and lead – asking, in effect, that you become a *canvas* on which you will allow me to paint a fresh picture of what I have found leads to creating and maintaining a higher performing organization. I know that as an executive you have read and heard a great deal and yet still search for something to believe in. My hope is that you will find the learnings now shared with you as credible, actionable and impactful in a positive way on you and your organization.

As you are probably well aware, the literature is replete with examples of failures – whether Marconi, Enron, Tyco, Lehman Brothers, Royal Bank of Scotland Group, Kodak, Blackberry or others. On the other side, that same literature is full of great organizational stories as told in books such as Jim Collins "Good to Great", journals, magazines or global studies by think tanks, academics or consulting organizations. These often describe the most innovative organizations; talk about the most admired organizations or best places to work; organizations with the best CEO's; Baldrige Performance Excellence and EFQM Business Excellence winners and more. In my opinion organizations like Nestlé, P&G, Ford, Apple, Google, Gortex, Tata and a few others (disappointing that there are not thousands of them) are excellent examples of enduring organizations which have set the standard for others to follow. In this volume, I will share my hands-on experiences as a senior consultant around the world. The examples will come from the many organizations I have worked with or worked for over the years.

The real question that I believe needs to be addressed by business schools is:

> *What does it take to build and maintain a truly enduring and continuously successful business – one that stands the test of time, turbulence and change and despite all that has continued to set the standard for performance and excellence by which other organizations are measured?*

As the author I am absolutely convinced regarding one critical point after my years of experience: **90%+ of the cases when you find even a good organization under-performing or an organization that has failed, the root cause is a failure in leadership.**

Chapter One

Charting Your Destiny with the Business Model

It has been said that "good things often come in small packages." It is my sincere hope that this is the case with Volume I of this series of short Strategic Briefings for Executives which can help you and your leadership team build and maintain a higher performing organization. This series is dedicated to those of you who are firm believers in the vital importance of life-long learning and improvement – for yourself and your organization.

Before getting into more detail, let me ask if you and your leadership team have ever stepped back and asked yourselves these questions:

1. What really makes our organization unique? What really distinguishes us in the minds of our customers or other key stakeholders – makes us stand out in a way that motivates customers to *want* to do business or have a relationship with us rather than a competitor?

2. What are those most important factors which form the foundation of that uniqueness and our competitiveness? These are the factors which if nurtured and developed effectively and consistently can lead us to creating and maintaining a great and enduring organization – one which can stand the test of time and turbulence and through it all lead by example – setting the standard of excellence and long-term performance by which others in or even outside our industry are measured and through which we have ensured creation and delivery of value to our key stakeholders continuously – value which they recognize and appreciate resulting in exceptional relationships being created and maintained with them.

Let's now begin to build the simplified model which I believe captures all the critical factors which will ultimately determine your success as an organization. It has five major components which follow a Deming plan, do/execute, measure and improve cycle. These components, in their entirety, will define how your business operates and whether you, as the leadership team, are doing the right things for the organization. Your organization's business model and principles of engagement set the stage for how your organization will present itself to all of your key stakeholders including society.

The Business Model is the focus of this chapter:

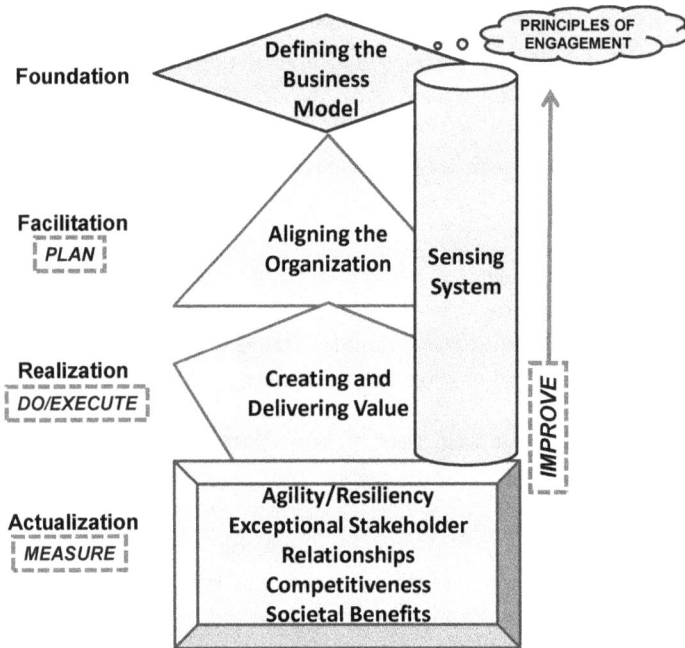

The primary output of the business model, as we will soon discuss, is your vision. However, to achieve the vision, you must align the organization's capability to harness first and foremost its human resources and ensure they are acting as all one team moving toward achievement of the common goal of realizing the vision. Everything your organization does should revolve around creating and delivering value to your key stakeholders. In my opinion this is the true purpose of a business. As you move forward you need to ensure that you have the best *sensing system* to monitor not only internal progress toward goal, but external changes such as evolving trends, competitive activity, changing customer requirements and more. This will allow your organization to be more agile, more resilient and be able to make any mid-course corrections necessary to stay on track toward the goal. If the above are done and done well, the four outcomes shown (and others as discussed in Chapter 7) should be within your grasp.

GETTING DOWN TO BUSINESS — THE "BUSINESS MODEL" THAT IS!

There is no strong consensus over what a business model is or isn't. There have been a number of misconceptions about its key components and its power to create either an enduring organizational success story on the one hand such as Proctor and Gamble, or one that has to be rescued from bankruptcy such as General Motors.

Wikipedia's *business model* definition is so bland as to be meaningless:

> *In theory and practice, the term business model is used for a broad range of informal and formal descriptions to represent core aspects of a business, including purpose, target customers, offerings, strategies, infrastructure, organizational structures, trading practices, and operational processes and policies. The literature has provided very diverse interpretations and definitions of a business model.*

Let's begin by asking why, in the diagram on the facing page, the business model is referred to as being the **Foundation**? The answer is because the capability of the leadership team to design each of the components of the model and to then achieve *fusion* among them will ultimately determine whether you create an enduring organization which sets the standard for others or whether your organization will die an untimely or premature death or simply live its life out as an underperformer. It's that simple. The organization, to survive and prosper, must be built and operated on a strong foundation. The business model, in this author's opinion, *is* that foundation.

Hewlett Packard was once described as "the company with a shining soul". If an organization can be said to have a soul then, quite simply, it is the business model. This model – its components working in harmony – blended or orchestrated expertly by the leadership team will create the *spirit* of the organization which will lift it and its people higher than ever thought possible. Being the foundation of the organization it needs to be rock solid – robust and unshakable, even when the equivalent of a tsunami hits!

CRITICAL COMPONENTS OF THE BUSINESS MODEL

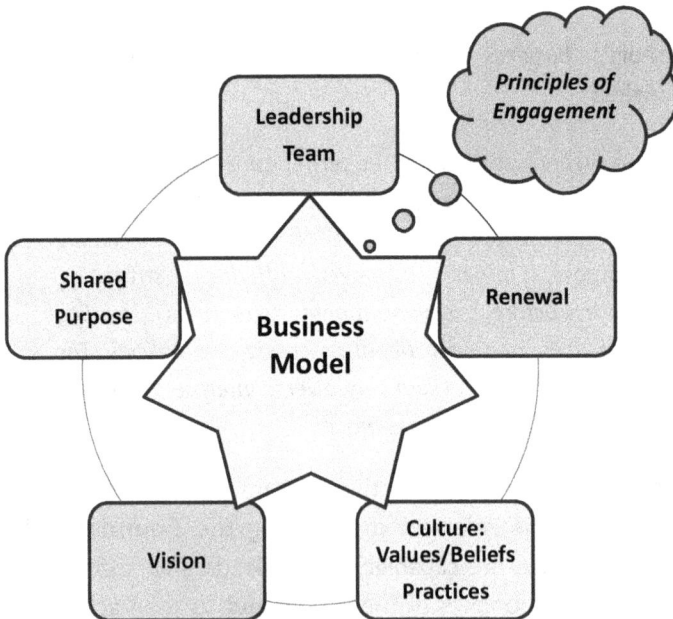

LEADERSHIP TEAM

The first among these components is the **leadership team**. The top team must design, drive and reinforce the organization's business model and what it represents on a daily basis. Here are some of the characteristics of a winning team which I have observed over the years:

1. The leadership team needs to be balanced, comprised of people with different complementary skills and interpersonal styles — the outcome being a synergistic effect. Diversity can be powerful — gender as well as cultural and international experiences can lead to more optimal decisions being made with greater regularity.

2. The team must be well connected to the rest of the organization, not isolated in the top floor c-suite but out engaging staff and stakeholders — listening and learning and then acting on the information they gather.

3. The team must be cohesive and must stand together (all one team) when difficult decisions are to be taken.

4. There must be a "one for all and all for one" attitude. Any problem of any single top team member is a problem for all top team members as it affects the organization and its performance. Everyone on the Management Committee must be clear that their number one objective is contributing to the success of the organization — not focusing on personal success. The heroes are those who are able to make the greatest contribution to overall organizational success.

5. All team members must be passionate about the organization's values and act as role models or exemplars.

6. There needs to be *joined up* thinking among all members of the senior team. This does not mean that a group of *yes* men and women is desirable — rather some creative friction is most desirable.

7. Embracing change, other points of view and diversity is an attitude essential to enabling the full value of teamwork at the top to be realized.

8. Communication, coordination, collaboration and the will to do so are keys to achieving higher performance among the top team and better ensure that the top team really is a team!

How would you and each member of the leadership team rate yourself on these eight attributes using a 1-5 scale where 1=poor and 5=excellent?

SHARED PURPOSE

The second component of the Business Model is the **Shared Purpose** – your organization's raison détre (the reason it exists in the first place). Every organization exists for a purpose. Is it compelling? Is it inspiring? Does it help attract the right talent to work in your organization? These are some of the critical questions you should be asking and answering.

One of the greatest business leaders of the last century, Bill Helwett, in a famous speech said:

> I want to discuss why a company exists in the first place...I think many people assume, wrongly, that a company exists simply to make money. While this is an important result of a company's existence, we have to go deeper and find the real reasons for our being...We inevitably come to the conclusion that a group of people get together and exist as an institution that we call a company so that they are able to accomplish something collectively that they could not accomplish separately – they make a contribution to society.

Then, of course, that purpose must be shared throughout the entire organization – reinforced regularly. Your people must believe it – must be uplifted by it as it will often speak to the desire of the organization to achieve outcomes of greater good for society – NOT just generate profits for shareholders.

> Tomorrow's company is clear about its distinctive purpose and values...it defines its purpose in a way that inspires whole-hearted commitment to achieving goals which are shared by all those who are important to the company's success. Tomorrow's company communicates its purpose and values in a consistent manner and acts in a manner consistent with its statements.

> RSA Enquiry, Tomorrow's Company, London, U.K.

In summary, the shared purpose is like the *anchor* that keeps your *ship* from drifting. In business there are many distractions – many opportunities or supposed opportunities which some executives would like to chase after. The problem is that this can dilute the power of your organization and be confusing to your people making it more difficult to achieve meaningful forward progress. In fact, "Lack of constancy of purpose" was found to be one of the "7 Deadly Sins of Management" in a research study conducted by me among CEO's. It is a practice which was identified by these CEOs as being lethal to the future success of the business.

In closing this section the following quote reinforces a key point:

> *Almost nothing in economics is more important than thinking through how companies should be managed and for what ends. Unfortunately, we have made a mess of this. That mess has a name: it is 'shareholder value maximization'. Operating companies in line with this belief not only leads them to misbehavior but may also mitigate against their true social aim, which is to generate greater prosperity (for society).*

Martin Wolf Financial Times August 2014

CULTURE AND SHARED VALUES

Continuing, the third component would be the **Culture** – particularly the set of shared beliefs and values.

Be aware that the culture you and your leadership team help create and reinforce can become either the greatest enabler of all your efforts to achieve success or the greatest inhibitor to that success. This is one you have to get right – period! And being a role model – leading by example, living the values of the organization isn't just important – it is critical to success!

Some organizations remain true to the ideas about purpose and values first set out by a visionary leader from the past – usually the organization's founder. One such example is Ove Arup, founder of the global civil engineering firm Arup.

In 1970, Ove Arup spoke at a meeting of his partners from around the world. The talk that he gave has become known as the Key Speech and in it he stated the aims and principles that guide the organization:

- We must strive for quality in what we do
- We should act honorably in our dealings with our own and other people
- We must aim for prosperity of all our members

From time to time members of Arup have asked whether what Ove said in 1970 remains valid. On each occasion they have found that it does.

Again, the values and beliefs of an organization should drive the behavior of individuals at all levels and in all parts of the organization. These behaviors should be the ones which senior management strongly believe will enable the achievement of success – accomplishment of those things most vital to the long-term future of the organization.

It is suggested that the number of values not exceed five based upon experience. The easiest thing in the world is to develop a *laundry list* of values/beliefs. Then it not only becomes difficult for anyone to remember them all, but even more difficult to operationalize them in your organization especially in your recognition, performance evaluation and reward systems. The key is identifying, always, **the vital few most important ones** – the ones which you and the leadership team and your people believe represent the greatest enablers to achievement of your vision. Often, as well, once you increase the number of values/beliefs beyond five, it can increase the likelihood that they will not be mutually exclusive, but too interrelated and therefore making it that much more difficult to operationalize them. Each value must be clearly defined and understood and the behaviors which support it as well.

Just to reinforce this idea, allow me to share an actual example from a client organization — a SME (small and medium sized enterprise) and systems integrator in Eastern Europe which has, in the past 18 months, grown successfully from 90 to 200 people.

Here is an actual example of one of the values and associated behaviors which the senior management team developed in a facilitated session:

People Make the Difference

In our organization, people are our most valuable asset. We can only be successful by having highly motivated, enthusiastic, involved and committed people. We support our people to reach their full potential and acknowledge their contribution to the overall success of the company.

Behaviors we look for from our people at all levels, including our executives who must lead by example, are the following:

1. We really know how to effectively motivate our people to do their best and gain their commitment to help our organization be successful
2. We always acknowledge and show appreciation for a job well done or for that little extra effort which our people often put forth
3. We make certain that in our organization we formally recognize people consistent with their level of achievement using a fair and objective approach
4. We ensure that our people are given the training and development they need and want so that they feel confident about their work
5. We invest in our people to help them achieve their full potential
6. The approach in our organization is one which involves our people – having them participate in new initiatives, collaborating in resolving issues of common concern and improving our work environment
7. We always make certain that we are available to support our people and to coach or advise them whenever they need help
8. We make a regular practice to listen, learn and act on feedback from our people so we can then eliminate barriers to their performance
9. We all show a willingness to give that little bit extra with no hesitation whenever it's needed for the success of the company.

Please note that the first key to success in creating an enabling culture is to define the right values. Once senior management has developed an initial set of values, they should be discussed with people in the organization to gain their feedback and suggestions.

The next step is to define the values and do so in a way that ensures complete commitment and understanding by each member of the leadership team. In this way, each member will be able to reinforce that value consistently among the people of the organization in all communications and actions.

The last step is then defining the behaviors that must be observed by any individual in the organization in order to identify them as a role model. The Human Resource systems (e.g., recognition, performance evaluation, and reward) of the organization should be geared not just to the issue of achieving targets, but *how* those targets are achieved namely, not leaving a trail of dead bodies behind in a zealous attempt to hit the target. These behaviors, for example, should be incorporated into any 360 degree feedback approach used by your organization.

RENEWAL

The fourth component is something called **Renewal**.

Renewal is defined as the "seamless and continuous integration of innovation, adaptation and learning". It is what will keep your organization from repeated engagements of ad hoc firefighting in reacting to changes in the business environment or crises requiring major change on a cyclical basis. In essence, renewal ensures continuous change.

What renewal does also is to ensure that your business model stands the test of time – it never goes out of date and through it all your organization is able to maintain a standard of performance by which others are measured. Your business model is continuously reframed, redefined, refreshed, re-energized in this renewal process. So few organizations get it right. Proctor and Gamble and Nestlé get it. Ford Motor Company got it. Apple and Amazon certainly get it. Why not you? Kodak didn't and went belly-up into administration after 120 years. Blackberry almost a similar case, Nokia, Sony and, well, the list goes on.

Part of the problem is that many times senior management can't let go of what they believe has been the key to their success historically – they can't move on in their thinking.

VISION

The last component of the business model is the vision – that destination you want your organization to reach more than any other – a vivid and compelling picture of a better or ideal future state. Think of it this way. Would a pilot take off from Heathrow or a cruise liner depart from Miami unless the captain knew the destination? Of course not.

Let me share an example of how I helped the management team of a StoraEnso paper mill in Dusseldorf, Germany define their vision. I simply asked them the following questions: "If I came back to this paper mill three years from now, what would I see? What would be different? What would be the same? What would you like to see or like to be doing here when I return?"

At that time the management team had never been challenged to think about creating a desired future state for their operation. They were energized as a result and came back the next day with an exciting vision of what they would like to see three years from then. This vision became their *beacon of light* to guide their subsequent actions, decisions, initiatives, resource allocations and objectives.

And please – no confusion between mission and vision! You need both. But vision is strategic and mission is operational. The mission is what your organization does day-in-and-day-out – it relates to the customers and markets it serves, the products, service and support it sells. It is the here and now – not the future destination.

It should also be said that at least annually the vision should be revisited and fine-tuned if necessary to reflect changing conditions, turbulence or other factors of critical importance to the future of the business and its direction. More on the vision in the next chapter on Alignment. Although, just to move the discussion in the desired direction, here is an actual example of the vision from that SME systems integrator client referenced above in the discussion of values:

> ### *Vision Statement*
>
> Our organization will be recognized in the next three years as a small giant providing innovative, secure and reliable services and solutions which will be available through the cloud technology to the worldwide market.

Once again, to be successful, there needs to be (1) buy-in from all members of the leadership team as well as a common understanding of what this statement means and how to achieve it; (2) it should reflect employee inputs and should be a source of pride and excitement – inspiration for all; and (3) there should be some time frame specified.

PRINCIPLES OF ENGAGEMENT

While more will be said on this in Chapter Seven, suffice to say that every business organization should have guiding principles related to how it intends, over time, to conduct itself, engage the community and society at large and set an example for others inside or outside their industry or sector. The areas of focus among these include but are not limited to sustainability and environmental responsibility, corporate social responsibility – issues often related to those identified by the United Nations in the Millennium Study as well as ethical business dealings and governance.

SUMMARY QUESTIONS FOR SENIOR MANAGEMENT BASED ON THIS CHAPTER

Answering the following questions should represent an opportunity for you and your Management Committee (that is, the leadership team, abbreviated MC) to learn and apply concepts regarding Chapter One:

1. Have you and each member of the MC described your business model — including each component and the value that component has to the long-term success of your organization?

2. Have you been true to your purpose — your reason for being as an organization by the decisions you have made in your MC meetings? Has that purpose kept you from drifting into unchartered waters or being distracted by what seemed to be opportunities, but ones which were high risk or did not represent doing the right thing for the business?

3. Why should anyone be led by you and your leadership team? What special qualities, talents, expertise or value do you bring to your people and your organization that can make them more successful?

4. What are your followers looking for from you — their expectations of you? Do you know? Who is following you? Your people? Your stakeholders? Others (e.g., competitors)? How can you find out?

5. What is it about your purpose, vision, beliefs, behaviors, practices and principles of engagement that will excite your people, catch their imagination, inspire them to reach a higher level of performance, motivate them to want to build an ever stronger emotional attachment to your organization? Do you know? How can you find out?

6. Can you in fact say that your leadership team is all one team — an example for how teamwork should work in your organization? How do you know? How can you improve?

7. What do you as CEO or member of the MC do each day (e.g., behaviors, practices) to send a clear message to your people that the customer is important? That the employees are important? Where can you improve?

8. If you think of the leadership team of your organization as a chain, what is its weakest link and how do you fix it to ensure it becomes an unbreakable

chain? What is its strongest link? What is the one behavioral characteristic of members of your MC that could be most problematic — holding you back?

9. Do you as CEO and every member of the MC maintain an idea book into which the answers to the following questions are completed at least once per week and then at the monthly MC meetings these are shared in a disciplined and prioritized manner?

    a. Based upon what I learned this week/this month, what is the most important improvement my organization needs to make to be more successful?

    b. Based upon what I learned this week/this month, what is one thing I can do to make myself more effective?

    c. How has my thinking changed this week/this month on any topic of particular relevance to the future success of our organization? How will that enable me to be a better change agent in my own organization?

    d. If I only had five minutes to talk with my Board, what would be the most compelling, most important ideas and issues I must tell them based upon what I learned this week/month?

    e. What were the *wows* for me — the most significant learnings from this week/this month?

    f. What new ideas do I have that I would like to implement in my own organization as a result of what I learned this week/this month? What do I think the benefit of doing so will be — the value added for my organization as well as holistically for the total organization and how would I measure it?

10. Have your own behaviors been consistent with your values/beliefs so that all of your people see you as leading by example — being good role models for them and your organization? How do you know? Where can you improve?

11. Are your Human Resource systems aligned at all levels including the leadership team to reinforce the behaviors and practices consistent with the values/beliefs of the organization? In particular, do your recognition, performance evaluation and reward systems balance achievement of hard targets/objectives with behaviors — ensuring that it is not just *what* you do but *how* you do it that counts most — minimizing collateral damage and avoiding leaving a trail of dead bodies in the zeal to achieve targets at any cost (the means always justifying the end)? What progress are you making and what has been the impact on the organization as a consequence?

12. Is the culture of your organization an inhibitor or enabler in achieving your vision? How do you know? Is it keeping your organization from reaching its full potential or being as competitive as you would like it to be? If so, what needs to be done to change it?

13. Have the decisions you have made today going to better ensure that you will get one step closer to realizing your vision and reaching your most desired destination?

14. How do you know if your vision really excites or energizes your people — giving them something to look forward to? Do your people know and understand the vision? How do you know they do?

15. How many of your people are strongly committed to your success in achieving that vision? How many feel confident that they know what contribution they need to make to ensure that success and that they have the capability to do so?

16. As a leadership team, would you make the "most admired" list in your industry? Why or why not? How would your people vote?

17. How do you define *innovation* in your organization so every employee has the same understanding? Is your approach to innovation a systematic one? What products, services, support, process improvements or other positive results do you have to show for your innovation? Do any of your values relate to innovation? Do your HR systems reinforce the importance and value of innovation to the success and competitiveness of your organization?

18. What was the last significant change in your operating environment to which you, as an organization had to adapt? Why should adaptation be important to you? How well do you (1) anticipate the need for change or (2) respond to the changes that are going on in your operating environment? Is your approach to adaptation a continuous one or do you take a crisis management approach? How can you improve what you do and how you do it?

19. How effectively have you as an organization learned over the past three years? What have you learned that has been of particular significance to the success of your business? How do you make certain that employees at every level and in every part of the organization are taking time for regular lessons learned sessions and recognize the benefits from doing so? How and where is this knowledge being captured? Who has access to it?

20. How well do you link and integrate #17-19 above? How do you know? Or, how can you find out?

21. Do you sense or detect any signals that indicate that change in your business or industry may be coming — change which will require you to create a state of readiness in your organization to address it effectively within the next 18 months? How well do you anticipate these changes? What have you learned from past situations that can improve what you do going forward?

Chapter Two

Planning and Executing through Alignment

Aligning the organization around the vision enables or facilitates not only the formulation of the most effective strategies, but also establishes the process through which those plans are executed effectively and efficiently.

Alignment is the focus of this chapter:

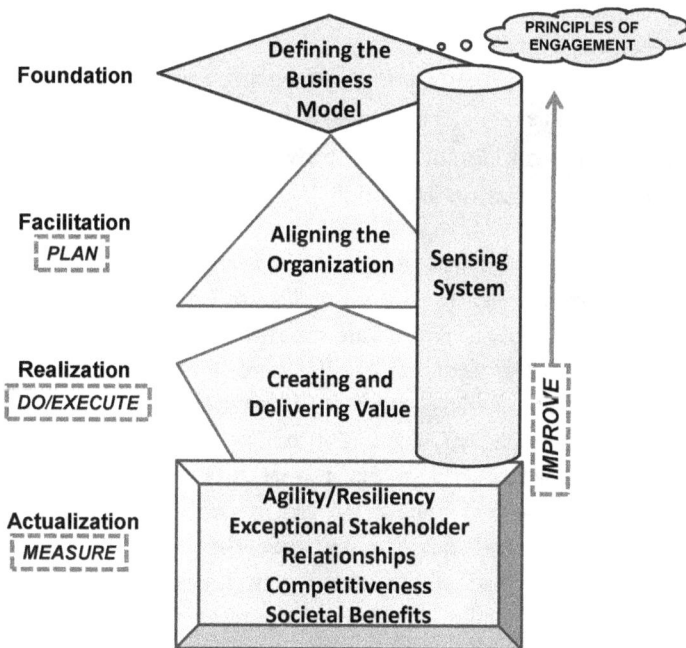

Foundation	Defining the Business Model	PRINCIPLES OF ENGAGEMENT
Facilitation PLAN	Aligning the Organization	Sensing System
Realization DO/EXECUTE	Creating and Delivering Value	IMPROVE
Actualization MEASURE	Agility/Resiliency Exceptional Stakeholder Relationships Competitiveness Societal Benefits	

MAKING THE VISION A REALITY

In essence, the vision can be considered the primary output of the Business Model and should guide the organization like that beacon of light in the fog that keeps ships from running aground. The vision should act as a litmus test (along with the purpose of the organization) against which all decisions, investments, resource allocations, priorities and initiatives are reviewed and legitimized. That is, in each case the question should be asked, "Are we being true to our organizational purpose and will taking this action move us a step closer to achieving our vision?" This is how you stay on track – focused and moving toward achievement of the vision.

Yet I have seen so many things go wrong in organizations over the years in this area. Here are a few of the mistakes I have observed that can diminish the power of creating a vision and aligning the organization around it:

1. The organization's vision is not on the employees radar screen – it is not even on management's radar screen! What do I mean? I have gone into so many organizations where I have challenged the Management Committee to write down their vision. Less than 10% can do it and usually only as a group effort – not individually. Sad – yes. An example of Lucite management? Put a plaque on the wall with a great sounding vision and that gets it done, right? Well hopefully if you put it in the reception area or lobby some of your customers will notice it and think it sounds great and possibly your employees as well! Too often the vision, like the plans or strategies, is developed as part of an esoteric process to which only selected senior managers are invited and then it is ceremoniously handed downward to employees.

2. The vision is not exciting or inspiring. Employees, customers and suppliers read it and begin to yawn.

3. Even if senior management knows the vision, they fail to communicate and continuously reinforce it with the people in the organization who are the very ones who ultimately must take the organization to that destination!

4. No one understands the vision — not even senior management! In going into the credit card operation of one of the UK's largest banks some years ago and talking to the employees, I found that no one really knew what the vision meant or the employees told me, "No, we don't do that around here". This is not at all uncommon in my experience. Or if you ask the Management Committee to come up with a simple way of explaining the vision to the people in their organization, each of the 15 members of the MC — or however many there are — will interpret it differently!

5. Senior management is unsure about what it will take to achieve the vision — oh no, we've created a monster! They are also unsure regarding the timeframe in which they hope to achieve it.

6. Senior management has not communicated what they expect from employees and therefore the employees are uninformed about what their contribution needs to be to help achieve it. Or senior management simply ignores trying to reach the hearts and minds of employees and instead takes the Neanderthal approach of command and control, in effect, substituting autocracy for leadership: "Around here we pay you to work, not to think. If you can't get the job done, then we'll get someone who can" — people after all are just tools, right? When management asks them to jump, their only response should be "how high?"

7. Senior management has not ensured people in the organization have the capability or requisite competencies they need to help achieve the vision.

8. The members of the leadership team themselves have not bought-in 100% to the vision and therefore are not 100% committed to making it happen.

Previously it was mentioned that some original research was done in the UK and Ireland called the "7 Deadly Sins of Management". It is interesting to note that CEO's and Managing Directors interviewed agreed that "lack of a vision and alignment of the organization around that vision" was the number one most serious failure of senior management – guaranteed to ensure the organization under-performs or ultimately fails.

CRITICAL COMPONENTS OF ALIGNMENT

For more details on the alignment methodology you may also view my Webinar conducted for the Madinah Institute in Saudi Arabia this past year entitled, "Magic, Myth, Madness or Just best Practice Methodology".

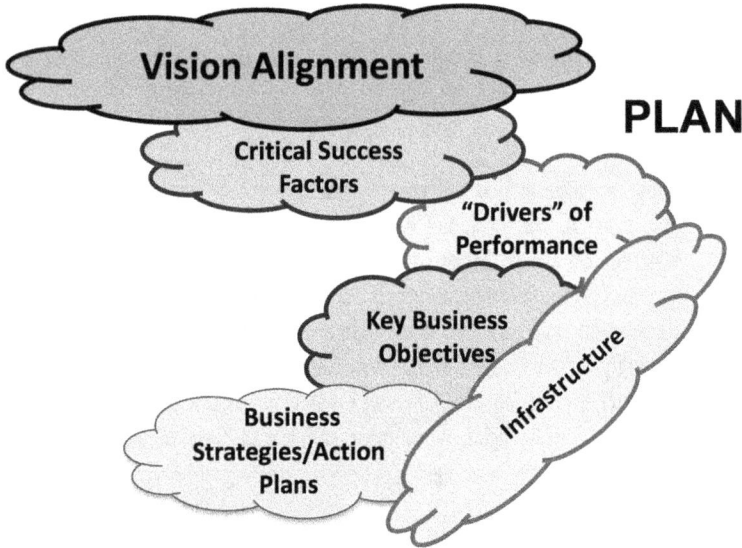

Please note that this is the part of the model where the planning is done – both formulation as well as the execution of the plan. Consequently it is essential that it be done and done right for the sake of the business now as well as for the future. The right things need to be done for the business – not just those things which make the organization look good on paper or to the financial markets, shareholders and investors or ensure larger bonuses for senior management.

The first element of **Vision Alignment** is determination of what are called the **Critical Success Factors** (CSFs).

There are two easy ways to think about critical success factors – those factors which will ultimately determine whether you will succeed or fail at achieving your vision. Here they are:

1. Talk with your Management Committee (MC) members and ask each one of them to identify those things which your organization must do and do right day in and day out in order to achieve the vision. Or, on the flip side, failure to do any one of these things right may well jeopardize the organization's ability to achieve the vision. Then share among your team and come to agreement. Ideally you should have three to five critical success factors (CSFs). In fact fewer are better but with an absolute maximum of five to seven. Try to get focused. Look at issues of interdependence between the ones you identify as there may be overlaps. Try to keep them as mutually exclusive as possible — it won't be entirely possible as everything in one way or another, large or small, links to everything else. These will tend to be relatively high level factors. This is NOT an exact science; OR

2. Again, discussing with your MC, have each person identify those items which they believe to be the most important factors the organization MUST focus on, invest in or emphasize continuously to achieve the vision — relentless pursuit would be a good phrase. Again, share and come to agreement — 100% agreement! And 100% commitment.

Often in practice, these CSF's are areas such as "providing innovative solutions" or being "intensely customer and market focused" or making "people make the difference" a reality in the organization by investing in your human assets — generally high level domains, which in the second step we will start to get underneath.

Another good exercise, from experience, is to ask each member of the MC what contribution they individually as well as the part of the organization for which they have responsibility can make to each CSF. While this will become refined as you go through the process, it begins to move the organization, at least at the senior level, toward establishment of ownership and accountability early in the process. It also ensures that you are working as all one team toward a common goal, namely achievement of the vision and focused on doing what's best for the overall organization.

It may also be instructive to ask the MC members for their opinions as to the barriers or vulnerabilities which could prevent attainment of the vision and come to agreement on how to mitigate them.

Here once again is an example from the SME system integrator referenced in Chapter One. These were their critical success factors:

> ### *Critical Success Factors*
>
> - Powerful business development
> - Excellence in human resource management
> - Strategic stakeholder management
> - Enterprise resource planning
> - Operational excellence
> - Continuous improvement, innovation and learning
> - Alignment with our organization's vision

The second component of Alignment I like to refer to as **Drivers of Performance**.

The CSFs are high level – more strategic in nature. Now let's drill down a bit to get to those areas which can be more easily acted upon and around which plans can be also more easily and clearly formulated. This will make the process of moving forward and achieving the vision more manageable. So, the challenge here is that you and MC members must ask themselves the following question:

> *Looking at each CSF, what would you say are the one to two factors preferably which, more than any others, drive or will drive our performance as an organization in each of those three to five critical areas identified above such as providing innovative solutions or continuous improvement, innovation and learning?*

You do not want more than three factors or drivers so prioritize, prioritize, prioritize. Here the focus must be on the absolute essentials – the vital few not the *nice to haves*. Again, ultimately you must set objectives and define strategies. You can easily end up with 20 or 30 if you are not careful. With this number, it is humanly impossible for an organization to achieve forward traction as there just not enough resources available to make it all happen. *Focus!*

Examples include "talent management/succession planning" or "employee engagement to ensure higher emotional attachment and commitment" or "designing specific relationship strategies for the top ten most important accounts or most important strategic stakeholders" or "design and implementation of a customer and supplier lab to test new innovative concepts and gain additional ideas for differentiating our products and services or adding new ones to the portfolio". The list can go on, but a word of caution *no more than* three Drivers for each CSF please!

Once again, taking an example from my SME systems integrator, the drivers for one CSF (Strategic Stakeholder Management) were:

Strategic Stakeholder Management

- Build secure customer relationships by establishing unique relationship strategies which deliver exceptional value
- Carefully select strategic alliances and business partners – building and strengthening our working relationship and collaboration with them
- Align key business objectives and strategies with an understanding of stakeholder expectations and our goal of adding value in the relationship

Continuing, the third component would be the **Key Business Objectives (KBOs)**.

The purpose is not to take you through the basics of Key Business Objectives – how they need to be measurable, with specific, achievable, realistic and timebound. You've been there before and you are well beyond these basic issues. Once again, no more than one to two KBO's for each Driver of performance!

Otherwise you will soon have 30 KBO's and be unable to deliver on few of them due to the finite resources available.

The unfortunate thing is that many organizations will have, in fact, as many as 30+ KBO's. I remember going into Data General outside Boston and finding this to be the case. In asking if anyone knew whether achieving the KBO's would help them achieve the vision, no one had a clue. The KBO's had been developed in an isolated set of work activity without any reference to the vision. So one has to ask, "Why was the vision created in the first place if it was going to be ignored and if everything the organization was trying to accomplish was unrelated?"

Moreover, when I speak with senior management of a client organization I define *key* as meaning most important (strategically is implied). Or, if you like, the vital few. Does 30+ sound like the leadership team has identified the vital few? Not to me it doesn't. It sounds like we have some of the *mundane many* or *nice to haves* in with the most important ones. And as I speak to the management who has responsibility/accountability for achieving them, they are already shaking their heads in despair, having given up in advance at the daunting task ahead which they know cannot be achieved with the level of resources available. They see their bonuses evaporating before their very eyes – demoralized from the start. The fact is that too many KBO's can act as a paralyzing agent to your organization.

Unfortunately this situation tends to be the rule rather than exception in my experience. Why is it so hard for senior management to really identify the vital few? Maybe they are just *hedging their bets* in case they miss what's really most important and they figure if they shoot around the target there may be some splatter that hits the target? Maybe they really don't trust the judgment of their leadership team members? So, better to take a shot gun approach than a rifle approach, at least you may end up with something to show for it! Or maybe they just do not want to take the time to do it right – to arrive at ensuring the right things are done for the business – instead they just do *things* that are expedient. Please don't let this be you and your organization!

A useful exercise for the leadership team is to construct a matrix which has all your KBO's down the left hand side and all of your key stakeholder groups across the top. Now you and your team should go through each KBO and ask the following questions:

1. If we achieve this KBO, is it clear that because of the linkages we have created to the vision, that we as an organization will get a step closer to realizing that vision? Why or why not? If not, then what do we need to do about it?

2. If we achieve this KBO, which of our stakeholders benefits most? What is the benefit? Which groups benefit least – does that worry us? Are the benefits balanced – somewhat equally distributed across the stakeholder groups or are they biased toward one group? If the latter, what, if anything do we want to do to fix the situation or do we want to live with it? What are the consequences to the business long-term, if any, of leaving it as is – namely unbalanced?

3. Probably it is also worth asking each member of the MC what contribution each of them personally as well as their part of the organization can make to achieving each KBO – you are all one team, right? You sink or swim together. It is commitment time. Again here is where some sense of ownership and accountability come into play – take advantage of it! Understand the interdependencies! Make it work for the sake of the overall organization not just one part of it – be a team!

In terms of examples, here are some of the key business objectives for the Eastern European SME systems integrator organization we have been referencing. The KBOs are the ones that relate to one of the drivers mentioned above, namely "Build secure customer relationships by establishing unique relationship strategies which deliver exceptional value".

Key Business Objectives

- Identify, approach, and establish a relationship with ten target accounts which have been assessed as value oriented based upon our criteria (e.g., have a strategic orientation, want a supplier they consider as a valued business partner and is an organization that focuses on value added not price) in the next three to six months.

- For existing value oriented accounts, develop and execute a specific relationship strategy in the next three months for each of the top 15 (based upon our criteria) that will enable us to go deeper and broader within that account and ensure profitable growth over the next three years and beyond.

The fourth component is the **Business Strategies/Action Plans**.

Now, for each KBO, you need to define a strategy or action plan on how you will achieve it – something which you can monitor progress against as well as its impact on a monthly. It should have tasks identified, timing, ownership/accountability, interdependencies highlighted, potential barriers and how to overcome them and measures of success well defined. More about performance measures in Chapters six and seven. Again, these business strategies or action plans together should comprise the overall business plan for the organization.

Looking at the example of the SME systems integrator and now focusing on KBO #1 above (e.g., new value oriented target accounts), the following could be considerations for developing the action plan/strategy:

1. Who owns this KBO? Who can contribute most to its achievement?

2. Is there a need for a sponsor – a member of the leadership team or a domain Council (see discussion below in this Chapter regarding infrastructure) to act as a sponsor?

3. Should we form a cross-functional Strategic Business Improvement Team (SBIT) to execute the action plan/strategy? Who should be on the team? Who should be the team leader? How do we ensure we use this experience for development of people on that team? Is there a need for any further training/knowledge/learning to take place to ensure team members have the capability to succeed?

4. What are the steps which must be taken to ensure this KBO is achieved?

5. How do we ensure flawless and complete execution?

6. What are the timing of the activities/steps required for achievement?

7. What are the interdependencies? That is, what other groups (departments, functions, divisions, or even external business partners or suppliers) are we most dependent upon for ensuring we are successful in achieving this KBO?

8. What will be our measures of success (qualitative and quantitative indicators)?

9. How soon should we implement our quarterly relationship review process and gain feedback to determine how well we are doing in the eyes of our new account and how we compare to other suppliers they may be utilizing?

10. How will we assess the value we are delivering and to whom? Is it recognized?

11. How will we monitor progress? How often will we monitor progress/look for a status update? Who will be involved?

12. What do we perceive the barriers to achievement to be and how do we mitigate them?

13. What is the communication plan to keep our people and our stakeholders informed?

Just a quick word based upon my experience. Because of the extremely dynamic nature of markets today – the turbulence, it can be helpful to have an 18-month rolling plan with a three year horizon. This will not fit all situations! But if you review the plan on a trimesterly basis – looking at progress over the past three months (you still have monthly progress reviews against action plans and looking at measures of success) and then adding another three months out each time (to keep the 18 months forward and three year horizon), you may find that this can work effectively and efficiently for you.

Also, it is critical that the right questions be asked during the reviews. These reviews must not be interrogations, painful, or brutal exercises. They need to be constructive. Also, because the MC is all one team, one senior executive's problem is everyone's problem and potential suggestions and solutions should be sought from everyone on the MC. Too often one MC member gets caught in a difficult situation and his or her organization's performance is not meeting planned targets/objectives while the others just watch him or her struggle.

The last component of Alignment is the **Infrastructure.**

If you want to get your plan implemented as flawlessly and completely as possible and as efficiently as possible, you may need to consider having the right infrastructure. In other words, it is suggested that you create a selective number of Councils responsible for key plan elements – they become the focus and the owners – accountable for results.

It can be challenging, particularly in a national or global business, to get the whole leadership team together and get decisions on issues quickly even at the normal monthly review meeting so instead the suggestion is to establish four Councils as part of the overall approach to aligning the organization. Each Council will have a subset of the MC members – the CEO will be included in some of the Councils (one to two potentially) as well.

The focus is on speed and agility here as well as reducing the demand on senior management's time. Do not always pick the usual suspects as members of the Councils listed below – get some diversity of membership – diversity of thinking and experience. So, just as an example, the Human Performance Excellence Council may have the CTO or CIO as a member and so on. Don't be afraid to mix and match – it will work out for the best in the end – trust me! Sometimes it is useful to have the objectivity or someone asking the naive questions or playing devil's advocate which can cause people to rethink their positions or what they are about to do. So here are the initial set of Councils I suggest for your consideration:

1. **Human Performance Excellence Council** – anything and everything related to people – engagement, recognition, communication, building a community of trust, career planning and the list goes on. Making sure people are reaching their full capability to contribute to the success of the organization and that barriers to their success are being eliminated!

2. **Operational Excellence Council** – anything and everything related to business process, efficiency, productivity, 6-sigma/lean, and the list goes on. Making sure that the routine things get done and done right, first time, every time – reliability must be a top priority!

3. **Competitiveness and Growth Council** – anything and everything related to new product/service/support development and launch, R&D, innovation, learning, adaptability, agility and the list goes on.

4. **Relationship Mastery Council** – anything and everything related to building exceptional relationships with any key stakeholder group from customers to suppliers to the community and beyond – and some overlap with Human Performance Excellence as the leadership team needs to know how to develop exceptional relationships with the people in their own organization (as well as with stakeholders) – making their people want to be followers!

Each of these four Councils must be supported by a Strategic Business Improvement Team (SBIT) composed of three to five team members. They must be cross-functional and all should be high-potential individuals. Part of the purpose of this process is to develop these individuals and watch their performance so they can be moved into appropriate and higher level positions later on.

These SBIT members must now, often for the first time, take a holistic view of the organization – not just their departmental, functional or divisional view. They may need some training in basic skills such as process management, quality tools and techniques or others – so be prepared to provide it. They may also need help with their presentation skills as each month they will be asked to present progress and results to their respective Council. Their performance in this role must be considered in their overall performance evaluation for the year as well as in assessing their leadership potential.

Councils should meet once per month with their respective SBITs **and** there should be one combined meeting of all Councils once per month so that everyone has a chance to see, discuss and challenge progress and results.

Just as an aside, it is true that structure should follow strategy. It is also true that successful strategy execution is much more about process, people and culture than any other factors. It may well be that some of the initiatives or strategies needed to achieve the KBOs will require structural changes as well. If so, the SBIT supporting the appropriate domain Council can be very useful in terms of gathering insight and information, talking with others in the organization and laying the groundwork and support for change in a very participative and constructive way. The idea is to get out in front of any potential change and communicate, communicate, communicate and involve as many as possible in the change process.

Summary Questions for Senior Management Based on this Chapter

Answering the following questions should represent a learning opportunity for you and your MC regarding Chapter Two:

1. If everything you are about to undertake relates to achieving the vision, what are your plans to ensure the eight mistakes shared in this chapter regarding the vision are not made?

2. How do you ensure that every objective, strategy, resource allocation, initiative, priority or decision you and your leadership team make — as well as those made elsewhere in the organization at any level, are aligned with (support) your vision, purpose and critical success factors?

3.   What are the three to five most critical factors that you and the leadership team believe will enable you or better ensure you achieve your vision and realize greater success for your organization in the future?

4.   What contribution can you and each member of the leadership team (and their organizations) make to each critical success factor? How will you ensure those contributions are made?

5.   What do you and the leadership team believe will determine how successful the organization will be — the determinants of performance for each critical success factor (what I have called the drivers of performance)?

6.   Do you have one to two key business objectives for each of these drivers of performance? Is there 100% agreement among the leadership team? How strong is the relationship between each KBO and driver — small, moderate or significant? If not significant, is there another KBO that could be set that could have greater impact?

7.   How will achieving the KBOs enhance your competitiveness?

8.   For each of your Key Business Objectives (KBOs), answer the following questions: (1) If you achieve that KBO, who benefits most among all of your key stakeholder groups? (2) What value is created and/or delivered for each KBO achieved and for each stakeholder group identified?

9.   Have you established strategies and action plans indicating ownership/accountability, tasks, timing, interdependencies, measures of success and potential barriers?

10.   How will you ensure flawless and complete execution? What is your process to do so? What specific actions need to be taken (list the first three steps) to better ensure flawless and complete execution? How do you need to re-engineer your process to better ensure more complete and flawless execution?

11.   What infrastructure (Councils) have you established to better ensure execution? Have you ensured diversity within each Council or just picked the usual suspects? Have you identified one Council member as the sponsor for each KBO and associated Strategies? This individual would also be a coach to the SBIT for that Council.

12.   What criteria have you used to select members of the SBITs? How will you ensure the members of these teams are developed during the process? How

will you ensure that the performance evaluation of each team member is included in their annual appraisal, that these individuals all have a career path established for them and will be appropriately recognized for their contributions?

13. How will you identify and incorporate any structural changes necessary to maximize the impact of your plans and strategies on the organization's success and ultimately the achievement of the vision? How will you communicate the needed changes to your people early on and involve them in making the changes? Are you ensuring a maximum participation approach? Have you effectively assessed any potential barriers to change and how to mitigate them?

Chapter Three
Creating and Delivering Value
Part I

My observation is that *value* is one of those overused terms that has lost its true strategic meaning. The version of value often being used is what could be called a commodity definition, namely, "what you get for what you pay". Basically what is being said is that if you are a consumer (or stakeholder for that matter) and you purchase something from the butcher, the baker or the candle stick maker, you don't want to get ripped off! Well, there is a bit more to it than that – thankfully.

Creating and Delivering Value is the focus of this chapter and Chapter Four:

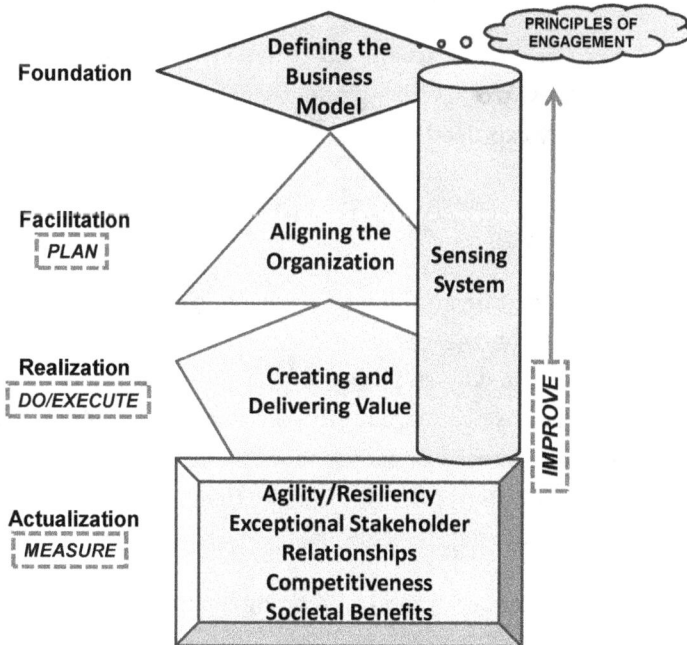

This chapter will be a longer one, emphasizing the compelling strategic significance of the *value* concept. It is my feeling that value is one of the single most important strategic concepts to evolve in the past 15 years. What I have gained from experience is that value is, from a customer perspective (or stakeholder perspective) the critical source of differentiation and competitive advantage. It is also the foundation of creating and maintaining exceptional stakeholder relationships.

Peter Drucker is one of the most revered management gurus. He once said that "the purpose of a business is to create a customer". For years everyone bought into that – and, frankly, it carried a lot of weight. However, it needs to evolve and now a more appropriate purpose for a business might be:

> To identify the customers it wants most, attract them and keep them by building exceptional relationships built on an appropriate value proposition.

That works well, but again, after even more experience in multiple cultures around the globe the resulting conclusion on this topic is now captured below:

> The true purpose of any business (or organization) is to create and deliver value.

In our model, creating and delivering value is right at the center. It is what should be the result of executing your plans, achieving your KBOs. This is why this stage in the model is referred to as the **Realization** stage. Again, if you are not realizing value creation and/or delivery as a consequence of everything you are doing – then you are not doing the right things for the business – which is what leadership is all about!

If everything your organization is doing – internally as well as externally does not involve in some way, shape or form the creation or delivery of value, you are in for a slow decline – one which ultimately could spell your demise. In his Harvard Business Review article, "What is Strategy", Michael Porter said, to paraphrase, "There are only two possible business strategies. The first is to do what everyone else does but do it better. The second is to create and deliver value with everything you do as an organization." The latter can lead to long-term success while the former can lead to becoming just *an also ran* or *flash in the pan* so to speak.

And, just to clarify, I am *not* speaking of **shareholder value**. This term has become a cover-up – a smoke screen for the zealous pursuit of profit. Organizations which focus intently on maximizing shareholder value are really focusing on maximizing short term profit and, not surprising, these organizations as a whole tend to underperform those who do it right – they have the right focus, a broader purpose and take a balanced approach which creates value for all their key stakeholders including the communities in which they operate. These same organizations are also undermining or jeopardizing their organization's long-term future by making short-term decisions that make them look good on paper or to potential investors while ensuring substantial bonuses for the top few.

In Chapter Two there was reference to creating a matrix of KBOs and Stakeholders and asking, "who benefits most – who receives value for achieving each KBO and what is that value?" This really should be a must do activity for the leadership team.

So, how should value be defined? You may or may not agree, but here it is based upon my experience:

> *Value is the sum of the tangible and intangible benefits*
> *perceived by the customer or other key stakeholders.*

As such, it is an immediate source of differentiation and competitive advantage for your organization. Some organizations find that while customers may indicate they are completely satisfied, when asked how you compare to others who offer competitive products or services, they say "we see no difference", in other words, there is nothing that distinguishes your organization in any meaningful way. This is obviously not what you want. Some of the key elements that deserve further mention are these:

- Value is measured in terms of benefits. For years Xerox saw satisfied customers defect, going instead to Canon or Ricoh or wherever they thought the grass might be a bit greener. The fact is that most customers are always asking the following question, "Why should I do business with you? What do I get from doing business with your organization that I wouldn't get elsewhere?" If they come up empty-handed, they often defect or at least spread their purchasing power between your organization and a competitor/alternative provider.

- The benefits have to be clear, recognizable and appreciated by the customer (or other stakeholder). It does not matter if you think your organization is delivering value. If the customer (or other stakeholder) doesn't perceive it then it is worth nothing.

How do you know you are adding value? When you reduce the customer's (or other stakeholder's) cost of doing business with your organization! And there are two costs which *must* be recognized and if either one is inappropriate, expect defections or declines in the quality of working relationships with key stakeholders! What are they?

- Economic — what it costs me to get the product, service or support I want from your organization.

- Emotional — how much pain do I incur to get the product, service or support I want from your organization?

You can have the highest quality product in the world at the lowest price and customers will still defect if they are experiencing too much pain in getting it or using it! For example while living in the UK I had British Telecom as my provider of telephone and internet services. One day I had what I considered a simple question I needed an answer to. Four hours later after calling seven different 800 numbers, encountering seemingly endless queues with repetitive messages, interacting with staff that obviously considered me an interruption to their daily activity – and, on top of it all, failed to meet their commitments to me, is it any wonder that my emotional index soared exponentially and I said to myself, "I *hate* doing business with this company!" Is that what is happening in your organization and you don't even know it?

Just keep in mind, and this point was made in an earlier chapter, the culture you create in your organization will ultimately become the biggest enabler or the biggest inhibitor to its success. The first place to start is by having the right values/beliefs and ensuring that you as the CEO or any other member of the MC are all role models for those values and beliefs – that every day and in every way your behaviors and practices reflect those values and beliefs and that you all clearly communicate and reinforce the importance of creating and delivering value.

VALUE – GETTING THE RECIPE RIGHT

While value creation and delivery is exactly what you want and need to be pre-eminently successful in the marketplace, you first need a foundation upon which to do it – a state of readiness so to speak!

The first ingredient that will allow you to get where you want to go is **Operational Excellence**. You have defined your CSF's, your drivers, set your KBO's and then defined your strategies/action plans. In each case, execution should result in value being created and/or delivered somewhere – either within your organization and between departments, functions, divisions, business units – that is, the internal customer or supplier community or externally with other key stakeholders – especially customers or end-users.

You see, in addition to value being the critical source of differentiation and competitive advantage for your organization, it is also, consequently, the foundation upon which exceptional customer (and other stakeholder) relationships are built and maintained. In my experience, however, value means little or nothing if you as an organization cannot even perform the basic routine things right on an almost flawless six-sigma level of operational excellence every day.

Let's take the case of key accounts – a B2B situation is easiest for illustration purposes. These accounts expect, and rightfully so, that such things as on-time invoices, correct invoices, on-time deliveries, complete deliveries, returned phone calls and emails (and the list goes on) will happen flawlessly and on a continuous basis.

Some years ago I was involved in research which was done with customers of Motorola. It was found that sales related problems were most destructive to the relationship B2B customers had with Motorola. In fact, 18% of customers said they would never do business with Motorola again because of the sales problem they encountered. What was the number one most destructive problem? Not getting their telephone calls returned! Why? Because if this happens it sends a very negative message to the customer that they are not important, that you are too busy with other more important things. And when you damage a working relationship between a client and their account manager, it is very difficult, time consuming and painful to recover – to win back the client's trust and confidence.

In another of my experiences, namely a division of Corning Glass which makes screens for laptops, the CEO of the Division and his management team flew to Japan to have a meeting with their number one account – Toshiba. The Corning CEO stood up in front of Toshiba's senior management team and proceeded to explain that they had come for the purpose of building a long-term and stronger relationship with Toshiba. When he finished, the CEO of Toshiba then stood up and simply told the Corning executive to sit down. The CEO of Toshiba proceeded to then state that "Your invoices are always incorrect and your deliveries are always late so why should Toshiba increase our dependency on Corning when you cannot even get the routine activities right?" Needless to say that was the end of the discussion.

You cannot create value for the customer if you are screwing up on the basics routinely or if customer expectations are that they bought the highest quality product available in the market and then these expectations are subsequently dashed on the rocks because of a product failure.

BUILDING ORGANIZATIONAL CAPABILITY IN CRITICAL AREAS

After Operational Excellence, the focus should be on **Building Organizational Capability** to create value and be capable of delivering it effectively through your products, services and support, with your organizational competencies as key enablers, through your human resources, in all your stakeholder engagements, and in all of your stakeholder relationships as shown in this diagram:

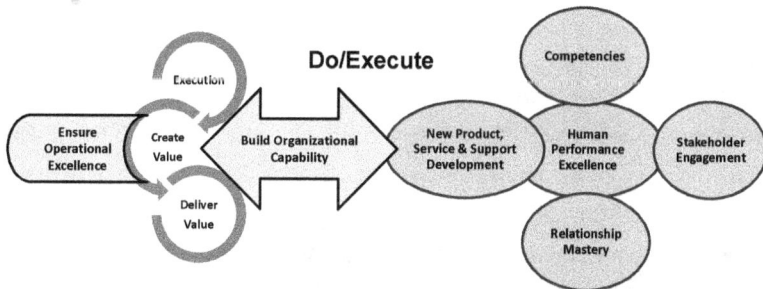

This part of the model is the **Do/Execute** part because this is where your plans and strategies become reality and you find out if they are really having the desired impact or not.

The second ingredient you should include to ensure you create and deliver value is related to your **Product, Service and Support Development Process.**

While Operational Excellence tends to focus on process and therefore applies also to your product, service and support development process, the critical point here is that the level of innovation you are able to integrate into the process – innovation driven by inputs from your people, customers and suppliers and by studying your competition as well can add tremendous value.

You need to design in, engineer in and, where appropriate, manufacture in value – **ALL innovation should result in value being added**. Ease of use and/or user friendliness are good examples. The thing about Nokia handsets and their software platform that set them apart was that the handset logic was common sense. One could learn to use the handset effectively without ever even reading the owner's manual which was often long and complicated. I saw firsthand how Sony overcame this issue of long and complicated owner's manuals by at least annually having a significant percentage of the agents from the Sony Information Center in New Jersey being brought together and asked about what the customers were saying to them regarding the owner's manuals as well as ease of use of their consumer products. Then the design, engineering, manufacturing and technical support groups would modify accordingly.

Not all features add value. In my numerous discussions and subsequent work with Compaq Computer, the feedback from the vast majority of customers was that they really didn't care if their laptop had a 50 gigabyte hard drive or a 100 gigabyte one because they really only needed ten gigabytes. And while research and my experience shows customers are willing to pay up to 20-25% more for what they perceive as true added value, they won't do it in a case like this. In fact, when Compaq asks more for their laptop because of it or the fact that it has a new processor that is five nanoseconds faster than the old one, sales can remain flat or even decline if the price remains unchanged or goes up slightly. The value is just not seen.

I also had the opportunity to meet with the CTO of Rodgers Cable in Canada some years back – the largest provider of internet and TV services in Canada. He was energized with the thought that soon Rogers Cable would be able to offer customers over 300 channels – at an additional cost, of course. Well, I don't know about you, but generally I view about five to seven channels and ignore the rest. Having 300 channels just complicates life and deducts value for me!

Let's take a couple of simple real life examples related to the Product, Service and Support Development process. General Motors, where I was employed for many years, is a standout – although not the only one when it comes to the issue of serviceability. Here the focus is on the time and effort car dealership service repair technicians must spend, the amount of time customers must wait as well as the cost of their repairs which can sometimes prove to be an unpleasant surprise. Many years ago, Pontiac Motor Division manufactured a small car called the Sunbird. Few people knew that when a customer with a Sunbird went in for a simple oil change, because of the way the engine compartment had been designed and engineered, the vehicle's engine had to be lifted up off the frame to reach the oil filter. The process took an hour and cost five times the normal amount.

You can talk also about the fact that the Chevrolet Cavalier and Pontiac Sunbird used virtually the same parts for everything in the drivetrain, but since these were two different Divisions of General Motors and all parts had unique part numbers, a dealer who needed a part for a Sunbird and did not have it but his counterpart in a Chevrolet dealership had it, the part had to be ordered from Pontiac causing unnecessary delays for the customer – even though the parts were completely interchangeable and could have been obtained within 30 minutes from the Chevrolet dealer nearby.

There are many examples from my experiences including such organizations as Electrolux, Boeing/McDonnell-Douglas and more. Unnecessary work for the employee, unnecessary time and expense for the customer! Value was being lost – big time! The thing was that the designers and engineers never spoke to any of the people who would have to service the car or the customers who would have to pay for the repairs! Instead they engaged in esoteric designs and engineering approaches which were the path of least resistance or they thought best as "they were the experts" – and then, of course enter manufacturing who needed things made easy to suit them on the assembly line at the expense of everyone else!

Continuing again, the third ingredient would be **Human Performance Excellence**. In the next volume in this series we will go into more detail on this topic. Suffice it for now that the focus is just on a few key points related to the issue at hand, namely value. The key questions here are simply these:

1. Is your organization one in which the primary focus regarding people is on obedience, and conformity to the rules and hierarchy? This marks your organization as one that is likely to be over managed and controlled – the 3C's (command, control and coordinate) are more than likely the philosophy. If this is your organization don't expect value creation and delivery to be taking place – it won't happen in a draconian environment (one in which there is fear and intimidation) where most employees have given up caring as they see they are being paid only to work and not to think. *or,*

2. Is your organization one in which the primary focus regarding people is removing fear and encouraging them to take initiative, learn from their mistakes, be creative and unlock their passion by turning them on – getting into not only their minds but their hearts as well and creating an emotional attachment to the organization? This is an organization in which people are being led and empowered. Now you have established the right foundation – built a compelling environment for having every employee creating and delivering value!

In order to build an organization that focuses on creating and delivering value, there must be excellent, continuous, 2-way communication between management and its people – transparency is key. Trust must be established and maintained. If these things are not there, you will get little traction in creating and delivering value.

Keeping the momentum, the fourth ingredient is related to the **Organizational Competencies**.

A few key points here. Think in terms of organizational competencies. What does that mean? It means simply that every organization has two different sets of competencies – one could be called *hard* competencies and the other *soft* competencies.

Most authors, academics and senior management for that matter most often focus on hard competencies. For example, one of Honda's core competencies is its technical competence in building small, highly efficient engines. In the case of Sony, it was *miniaturization*. Hamel and Prahalad's "Competing for the Future" has one of the best discussions on these hard competencies available anywhere. There is absolutely no question that these hard competencies enabled the organizations just mentioned to create and deliver value their competitors could not. As a result they enabled Honda and Sony to maintain a competitive advantage for many years. However, as discussed earlier, achieving competitive advantage and maintaining it long-term are two different animals. This is why successful organizations are focusing on developing longer-term, longer lasting competencies.

However, what is often overlooked are those almost hidden strengths – those *golden* threads that get woven into the fabric of an organization's culture – and which become part of its DNA over time. This issue was made clear during my research on the "7 Deadly Sins of Management" and my discussions with CEOs and Managing Directors in Western Europe. These strengths include, but are not limited to: innovation, customer and market focus, agility/resiliency, futures orientation and a few others. Each of these cultural predispositions or strengths enable an organization to create and deliver added value in new and exciting ways which can clearly differentiate them – distinguish them in the marketplace. Do you know yours? How are you leveraging them to create and deliver value? These also, in many cases, have a longer life than the more traditional core competencies.

Again, and this cannot be emphasized enough, your culture will ultimately determine whether your organization achieves its full potential – it will *enable* you or it will *inhibit* you.

The next ingredient needed for creating and delivering value is **Relationship Mastery**.

Almost everything you do as a member of the leadership team is dependent upon your capability to build exceptional working relationships. In their book, "Why Should Anyone Be Led by You", Goffee and Jones emphasize over and over again the fact that in their minds and based upon their research, leadership is all about relationships. Leadership without the requisite relationship mastery skills is at a significant disadvantage. I could not agree more based upon my experience.

However, beyond that point, you as the leadership team need to ensure you build this capability at every level in the organization. After all, who is it that day-in and day-out builds and maintains relationships with customers? Not you! It is your frontline personnel – sales, service, and technical support predominantly. What have you done to build their capability to do this exceptionally well?

Relationship mastery is the salient ingredient that ensures teamwork – communication, coordination and collaboration, working across business processes, functions and boundaries (real or imagined), making sure things do not slip through a crack because everyone is working together as all one team. This mastery extends to all activities with suppliers and other value chain partners and every other key stakeholder group. It needs to be pervasive or your organization will never reach its full potential for success. The internal customer and supplier concept needs to be alive and well and internal working relationships will also be their best if value is being created and delivered here also.

As an aside, it should be clear that as an organization, at least for your key strategic external stakeholders, you need to be developing unique relationship strategies one element of which encompasses understanding what value needs to be added to ensure that your customers and other stakeholder relationships will be secure. It is this security of relationships that provides an organization such as yours with added stability in times of market turbulence.

The last, but certainly not the least ingredient focuses specifically on enhancing the **Stakeholder Engagement** system. For purposes of illustration the customer will be utilized for discussion purposes although an engagement map can be constructed for each stakeholder group. In the case of the customer, the engagement map shows all the customer experiences whether sales, service, technical support, training, or whatever the interactions are that occur on a continual basis between your organization and its customers – in this case B2B.

Here is an example of the experiences which a Xerox copier customer can have in the course of doing business with them over time:

Managing the Customer Relationship: Xerox Customer Engagement Map

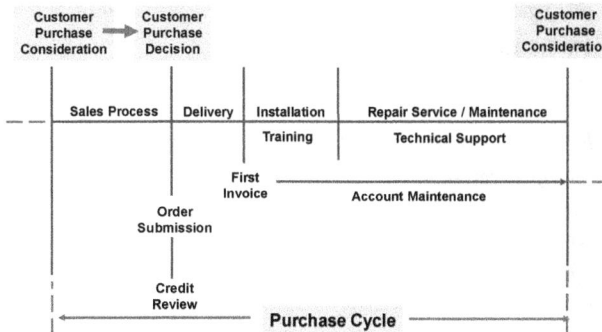

What are 6 Critical Questions You, Senior Management Need to Ask and Answer about this Engagement Map?

First, let us ask the fundamental question. Could you and each of the MC members draw this diagram – or even just list the comprehensive set of customer experiences that go on every day between your organization and the customer? Why not try it and find out?

The above diagram, by the way, would apply to many organizations – Motorola, ABB, Boeing and the list goes on. Of course there would be differences in terms of the specific details inside each of the individual experiences shown such as sales or technical support. Each of these, in themselves, is a customer facing **business process**.

So, what are the six questions you should be asking once you have the engagement map drawn? Here they are and let's see if you can answer them:

1. Which one or ones of these experiences are most important to your customers? You need to know that because, if anything, you want to be as flawless as possible in that experience – that's where you will get the greatest return from doing your best. Failure in that particular experience can be catastrophic and lead to customer defection almost immediately – remember the situation mentioned earlier with Motorola and sales related problems? In the case of Xerox, it was the repair experience. You know all too well what happens when the copier dies in an office. Fast and reliable repair service is critical.

2. What are the customer requirements – the basic routine things you need to get right day-in and day-out in each of these experiences (operational excellence)?

3. Where and how can you add value that will be recognized and appreciated (e.g., making it easier for them to do business with your organization) in each of these experiences? What is your plan to do so?

4. Where are customers having the greatest difficulties – most numerous problems in doing business with your organization on a continuing basis? What are you doing to uncover the root causes and take corrective steps to prevent their re-occurrence? What are these problems costing you in terms of lost loyalty, negative word-of-mouth or reduced purchases over time?

5. Where is competition doing a better job? What do they do and how do they do it? What information on this issue may be coming in through your contact center? Are you listening? What actions are you taking and how quickly?

6. Where do your frontline people have the hardest job satisfying the customer and why? How do you know? What do you need to do to better support them and ensure their success? How can you involve them, encourage and empower them to participate, take ownership and exhibit greater teamwork in addressing these issues?

By now you should be getting the picture. Take the time needed to understand the above engagement map for your organization – the return will be significant.

There will be multiple engagement maps – one for B2C, one for B2B, others for each stakeholder group. The suggestion is that you start with your customers.

In summary, what has been shared is what I have found to be the six areas (operational excellence; human performance excellence; the product, service and support development process; relationship mastery; competencies – especially soft ones, but not exclusively; and stakeholder engagement – especially with customers, but again, not exclusively as this needs to be done for your suppliers, business partners, community and other key stakeholder groups) where value can and should be created and/or delivered. Regardless of your organization most of these areas, if not all of them, should align with your Vision/CSFs and Core Purpose as well as being consistent with your values/beliefs. It's not rocket science or brain surgery – just common sense.

SUMMARY QUESTIONS FOR SENIOR MANAGEMENT BASED ON THIS CHAPTER

Answering the following questions should represent a learning opportunity for you and your MC regarding Chapter Three:

1. How do you currently define *value* in your organization? How does it compare to the definition given in this chapter? What changes in thinking are needed to bring your definition closer to the one given above?

2. How does your organization address shareholder value and how do you see it differently than the definition of value given in this book? How do you reconcile any difference between the two?

3. How well have you been able to reduce the customer's cost of doing business with your organization over the past three years, especially the emotional cost? How do you know?

4. Does your organization engage in a relentless pursuit of excellence, or are you complacent and satisfied to be just mediocre? Is there an inner tension — an inner restlessness of questioning by every member of the leadership team related to what you do; how you do; why you do it; as well asking what can be done better or differently tomorrow to strengthen the organization's performance? How well have you identified the basic requirements — those areas where your organization needs to be routinely flawless day-in and day-out — for each of your key stakeholder groups and in each experience they have with your organization? How well are you performing? What is your improvement plan and how will you ensure effective, efficient and complete execution?

5. What elements of your plan — your KBO's — are adding value (e.g., refer to the matrix of KBO's and key stakeholders), to whom and what value is being delivered? How do you know?

6. How do you create and deliver value through your products, services and support — in effect, design it in from the start?

7. How do you ensure you are bringing innovation that your stakeholders see and appreciate and which adds value? What sources of innovation are you utilizing (there are eight sources — customers, your people, competition, best practice comparisons/benchmarks, R&D, suppliers, crisis/impending regulatory change, focus on reducing cycle time).

8. How are you building the capability of your people to create and deliver value? What level of success are you having and how do you know?

9. How are you utilizing the creation and delivery of value to build exceptional relationships — part of your relationship mastery skill set (possessed by people

at all levels across the organization including the leadership team). How is this being utilized with all of your key stakeholders? What results are you achieving and how do you know?

10. What are your softer organizational competencies? Which ones can help enable creation and/or delivery of value to your key stakeholders?

11. What are you hard core competencies? Which ones can help enable creation and/or delivery of value to your key stakeholders?

12. What if starting tomorrow, your job as CEO or member of the MC was to help, encourage, ensure your people have the capability they need to reach their full potential to contribute to the success of your organization — to reaching that destination you have defined in your vision. What would you need to do differently or better individually and as a team to make that happen?

13. How effectively are you moving your organization from one which is managed and focused on compliance (e.g., obedience, diligence and expertise) to one where people are led, inspired, empowered and engaged so that the elements of human performance excellence, namely, taking initiative, being creative and releasing their passion is clear? Where are you now on the continuum from compliance to passion (reaching their hearts and minds) and what steps are being taken or being planned to move the organization to that better place?

14. How do you and leadership team believe the creation and delivery of value enabled your organization to gain competitive advantage? How can it help you maintain that advantage over time?

15. How effective on a scale of 1-5 where 1=poor and 5=excellent is your organization in creating value? How effective on a scale of 1-5 where 1=poor and 5=excellent is your organization in delivering value? What indicators are you using to tell you this is happening? What new sources of value could you utilize going forward and what would be required to make that happen? Which sources is your organization relying on most currently?

16. Overall, where do you believe your organization could do better or do more in creating and delivering value? What are you plans to make it happen?

17. How would the leadership team describe the role or value added of each of the following in helping the organization be successful? Rate (assess), on a

scale of 1-5 where 1=poor and 5=exceptional, how well you believe your organization performs (e.g., gets it totally right) in each of these areas:

- People (The leadership team included)
- Process (Including new product, service and support development)
- Information
- Communication
- Engagement
- Relationships
- Competencies

Chapter Four
Creating and Delivering Value
Part II

You may have been wondering, "OK, I understand that creating and delivering value should be fundamental to everything we do as an organization. But what are the specific factors that add value?" Below is a discussion of what I have discovered after years of experience around the globe about what seem to be the key sources of value.

NINE SOURCES OF VALUE

The conclusion so far is that there are nine components of value, illustrated in what can be referred to as the **Value Wheel**:

Recall our definition, that **value is the sum of all tangible and intangible benefits which the customer (or other key stakeholders) perceive**. Here, then are the nine areas where I have found value can be created and/or delivered.

BRAND, IMAGE/REPUTATION AND THAT *FEEL GOOD FEELING*

This is an intangible. It is something that produces what could be called a *feel good feeling*. It occurs when you as the customer, for example, believe that you are doing business with the best in an industry or product/service area or the product you have purchased is the best of its type whether an automobile, mobile telephone, computer or whatever.

In one of my executive development programs conducted for First Direct Bank at Leeds University Business School I had 40 top management personnel in the room with half of them being women. We were discussing the concept of value and just for fun I asked the women what car they would like to have in their garage. At once, they all said an Audi TT. Even before getting into their car – just looking at it there in the garage they felt good about how it looked and they imagined driving it in town – looking and feeling their best. That feel good feeling – an intangible source of value is power which cannot be overlooked except at peril! How many of your customers get a feel good feeling every time they do business with you or use one of your products?

BUSINESS PROCESS

There are several critical areas where you can focus your attention:

- Be easy to do business with. Keep it easy, simple, and uncomplicated – reduce or eliminate the pain for the customer or other stakeholders in obtaining what they need and want from your organization when they want it (e.g., accessibility, availability). During my work with ABB (Asea Brown Boveri) they thought it might be a good idea to go out and talk to key accounts — B2B customers who had stopped doing business with them. In so doing they found that in 70% of the cases, the primary reason given for defecting was that the customers found ABB too difficult to do business with — too time consuming, non-responsive, too much paperwork — in general, just too painful. The same point applies to consumer (B2C) markets whether DIY retailers, banks, rental car companies or clothing retailers to mention just a few. This is why, on average Bain and Company research has indicated there is as much as a 15-25% turnover in customers annually in most retail businesses. As you yourself have experienced many times, customers come up against unnecessarily complex procedures, lengthy or multiple forms to complete, pages of terms and conditions/fine print that they are expected to read and understand or unpleasant surprises including personnel who seem to see you as an interruption rather than the focus of their activity.

- Three critical parameters of any business process are quality, cost and cycle time. These are all interdependent. Simplifying a business process by reducing cycle time can actually reduce cost and improve quality — this is how efficiency can be approached in way that actually adds value. Why? Because fewer hands touch it — there are fewer operations and therefore fewer opportunities for defects to creep in and because there are fewer people and/or operations there is also less cost. Nirvana!

- Using technology in the right ways can both reduce the cost of supplying a service at the same time that it improves customer satisfaction (e.g., reducing waiting time) — examples include using technology as a substitute for human intervention (ATMs, automated toll collection, coin operated car washers) and limiting the range of service offers (e.g., restaurants with limited menus — just burgers, for example) and increasing the self-service options as in some retail stores. However, there is a delicate balance, depending upon the industry, between being high tech and high touch. Be careful not to lose the personalization that, where it is important, can be the key source of differentiation.

PEOPLE

People do make the difference when it comes to creating and delivering value. Frontline people and others such as account managers, technical support and more who serve the customer *are* the organization as far as the customer is concerned. Every welcoming smile, every smooth transaction, every thank you or show of appreciation can create value.

The eight pillars of service excellence

Attitude of Service	Show that you Care	Build Trust & Confidence	Show that you enjoy what you do
Be the best you can be – first time, every time	Be an Advocate	Show Appreciation	Show Respect

In my work over time I have found that there are eight factors, which more than any others, are valued most highly by customers – the ones that make the most difference and which can differentiate your organization from others. Get these right and your customers will get that feel good feeling each and every time they do business with you!

1. An attitude of service or willingness to help – no pulling teeth or *not my job* allowed
2. Showing that you care – empathy
3. Building trust and confidence
4. Showing that you enjoy what you do and enjoy taking care of customers – having fun (e.g., Southwest Airlines, First Direct Bank)
5. Be the best you can be – first time, every time – exhibit excellence, strive to be error free
6. Be an advocate for the customer – giving them the benefit of the doubt and/or taking initiative (being empowered) to do the right thing for the customer and the organization even if it means stepping outside your mandate or enlisting the help of others not in your part of the organization to make things right – *go the extra mile*
7. An attitude of appreciation (as the customer does not have to do business with your organization)
8. Showing respect

Motivating Service Personnel

A lot of discussion in the past has centered on the need for employees to be self-motivated. My response to this is **rubbish**. To me if I have witnessed an inadequacy of management from team leaders, supervisors, first line managers on up the ranks, it has been a distinct lack of understanding of the importance of motivating people and knowing how to do it. The idea is that together you can help lift the employee to heights of performance and contribution never before attainable. It means that you need to stop being a *policeman* and start being a *coach* and *teacher*. At a *minimum*, they need:

- To be satisfied with their working conditions, pay and fellow colleagues as a foundation
- To receive regular, frequent and constructive feedback about their performance and about how their performance relates to the level of customer satisfaction (internal or external)
- To be shown appreciation and recognition for outstanding performance – the latter being seen as objective
- To feel that they, as frontline people, are adequately supported and respected by those in other parts of the organization
- To feel that their own top management puts the customer first and leads by example in all they do related to the customer
- To feel that service is a team sport so to speak and that they are not only all one team, but are on a winning team
- To have the confidence and expertise that comes from being well trained and developed
- To believe that their learning curve is going up continually
- To believe that there is a future in the organization – that there is some career path and that they are not in a dead end job
- To believe that they are engaged in meaningful work activity – something that will make a difference for the organization, for the customer – not just engaged in mundane, repetitive or routine activity on a continuous basis, but instead activity which creates and delivers value

Service and sales personnel cannot operate well in an organization characterized by a Draconian management style (e.g., one characterized by fear and intimidation), a culture of blame and a rule bound system that leaves little or no room for discretion or initiative – where control and mistrust are the rule not the exception. In such an environment, empowerment will not work as people will be afraid to use it because they might get blamed if something goes wrong.

Some of the key value adding characteristics of your sales, service and technical people that I have determined in my work – ones which customers and other stakeholders recognize and appreciate include, but are not limited to:

- Being viewed as a trusted advisor or valuable resource
- Being viewed as being more technically competent than those of other providers
- Being able to provide innovative solutions
- Being proactive – anticipating problematic situations or identifying opportunities for the customer or other stakeholder
- Being seen as genuinely concerned for the welfare or success of the customer or key stakeholder
- Understanding the customer's or stakeholder's organization as well they themselves understand it – and much better than personnel from competition
- Being more responsive – always exhibiting an appropriate sense of urgency with customer or other stakeholder issues
- Taking a more consultative approach – not just taking an order for additional business
- Listening and learning – then acting on the information gained from the customer or other key stakeholder. Rule of thumb: 70-80% active listening, 20-30% talking

Another "critical to human performance" issue is the need to align your HR systems and processes to reinforce the behaviors and practices you want from your people. Key among these include: job descriptions, recognition systems, reward systems, and performance evaluation/360 degree feedback systems. The latter should incorporate the behaviors associated with your organization's values/beliefs which we discussed in Chapter One. Furthermore these mechanisms should be consistent. Too often I have seen that if an employee *gets a pat on the back* for a great job, they have no clue what they did and therefore would have a difficult time repeating that great job. In addition, I have found that far too often there is absolutely no consistency between the characteristics or content found in the job description, the performance evaluation, the recognition criteria or the values/beliefs of the organization as each one was developed in isolation from a blank sheet of paper. This is ludicrous and extremely confusing to employees.

PRODUCT

A prerequisite for being able to create and deliver value through your products is reliability and durability – namely products that are fit for use/purpose and last – they work first time, every time and keep on working. Maytag was well known for this and built a following among young wives whose mothers had had great experiences with Maytag appliances.

One key factor is being objective – gaining insight from customers, your own people and suppliers about the true competitive advantages of your products compared to competition or other substitutes.

If you are going to attract the customers you want, your products must reflect a design that catches their eye – appeals to them. User friendliness is another key to success and one that can add significant value compared to a product which is difficult to use. I remember returning my first Sony/Ericsson mobile phone because I found it just too difficult to use.

Packaging and presentation of products that shout *excellence* can add value. Here is an example from Lexus. Having owned a number of Lexus automobiles and having the chance to speak with dealer management over the years I found out that Lexus had determined that one of the very most important aspects of purchasing a new car was the delivery process. Customers who experienced a flawed or less than spectacular delivery process almost never came back to that dealership again. As a consequence, Lexus created a delivery show room and made the delivery a special event for the customer complete with a personalized training session.

User friendliness is an important issue – how long does it take the customer to become comfortable with use of the product or move up the learning curve to reach optimal usage of the product and its features? If it is too long or too painful, you are deducting value. It is here too that the integration of technology is key. Does the technology you have incorporated in your products enhance user-friendliness or deduct from it? Many organizations spend millions on a CRM IT (customer relationship management) system for their organization with great hopes. Often, however, people are able to grasp only a small fraction of the system's capability because the difficulty they have in using it and/or the lack of follow-up training that is done.

Again there are cross-overs here. The service and support of the product will greatly influence the customer's decision of future product purchases. A simple example. You may drive a Mercedes or other high end automobile, but the warranty service is problematic at the dealership (e.g., slow, unpleasant, ineffective) and that can reduce the customer's interest in repurchasing a Mercedes. In other words, the value of a product to a customer cannot be divorced from the standard of service and support that goes with it. The same for computers, medical equipment, weapon systems and the list goes on.

SERVICE

This element of added value requires an almost **seamless integration of innovation, people, technology and process** whether it is placing an order for office supplies, taking out an automobile loan at the bank, buying a pair of athletic shoes at an Adidas retail store, contact lenses at your local optician, buying groceries at your local market or D-I-Y materials at Home Depot or B & Q.

Simply ask yourself how many customer interactions take place in your organization every day? How many of these leave the customer breathless and panting for more? How many end up as a disappointment to the customer? It is here where the *eight pillars of service excellence* stated above as well as the factors that motivate sales and service personnel all come into play to ensure relationships are strengthened with customers and other stakeholders with each interaction or experience.

It should be kept in mind that research by the Service Quality Institute and Blogs by John Tschohi its President has shown that depending upon the service and industry, 40 – 65% (even as high as 86% as reported by McKinsey for banking) of customers will defect because of a bad service experience. Also, when looking for recommendations on where to do business, various market research studies have shown that as many as 67% ask their friends or colleagues. If those friends and colleagues give negative references as well as positive, your organization may either be a winner or a loser and not even know why. TARP (Technical Assistance Research Programs in Washington D.C. and their "Complaint Handling in America" study) has shown that a median of 16 others are told about a bad experience they have had while only a median of eight are told of a good experience. A Creative Conversations Blog by Peter Coffee indicates that nearly 70% of customers defecting as a result of a problem situation actually would have changed their minds and stayed if the problem could have been resolved in one call as opposed to multiple calls. I think you may be getting the picture!

The Service Profit Chain

Delivering a service often involves a sequence of interactions rather than a single transaction. Take the example of a going to a restaurant for a meal. Often you are welcomed by one person, being served a drink at the bar by another, giving your food order to yet a third person, discussing a wine selection with another and then being served by someone else and finally settling the bill with a cashier and collecting your coat from the cloakroom. So even in this simple example there could be as many as seven different individuals involved in your dining experience. Such a situation raises a number of issues:

- First is the fact that a chain of events or interactions is only as strong as its weakest link. An arrogant or rude wine waiter can destroy the overall experience and lead you to never coming back to that restaurant as well as ensure you spread negative word-of-mouth about the experience.

- The more people involved, the greater the probability of something going wrong — some lack of consistency in treatment of the customer which could lead to customer disappointment. In other words, specialization carried to absurdity can be damaging.

- Task specialization or lack of knowledge can also lead to customer frustration. The hostess is unable to tell you what the specials are on the menu that night or the waitress, when asked for the soup du jour, must go off to find out the answer when your expectation is that she should know. Or when you ask, "What do you recommend or what is the specialty of the house", the answer is simply "Everything is good" or "This is what we seem to sell the most of" — quite unhelpful.

- One invaluable resource is a book entitled "The Service-Profit Chain" by Heskett and others written in 1996. It is a timeless classic and should be read by every member of the leadership team. It quite clearly speaks to the tremendous bottom line impact on profits which service can produce when done right. "The Loyalty Effect" by Fred Reichheld of Bain and Company also provides similar insights.

Going Back to the Shop Floor

Perhaps one of the most effective ways to raise the standard of service – to determine where the opportunities for improvement might be is for senior executives to take a position, even for a day, as a frontline member of staff! At Virgin trains, senior executives take positions as conductors or other frontline personnel on a regular basis. From my personal experience executives at both Xerox and AT&T Universal Card Services (now part of Citibank) were required to take calls and handle complaints and requests for information from customers in their contact centers. The transformation in senior management thinking, insight and understanding gained from the interaction with customers and their own people can be profound!

There is a tremendous opportunity that results from getting it right in your call centers. These are often the highest volume points of interaction between your organization and the customer. From my personal experiences, allow me to share some examples. Siemens through their 95 contact centers around the globe receive more than 2.6 million contacts per year. The GE Answer Center in Louisville, Kentucky receives five million calls per year. AT&T Consumer Services when they won the Malcolm Baldrige Performance Excellence Award had 300 contact centers around the globe and every night the information collected from all of them was uploaded to a central computer at HQ and analyzed to identify changes, problems or opportunities. Compaq Computer had, at the time of my involvement, eight contact centers. These represent millions of opportunities annually to strengthen or weaken customer relationships – to ensure positive or negative references are shared in the marketplace as a result.

I recall a vivid situation with Dell Computer. I called the help line and was routed to a contact center in India. I tried speaking to a very nice young woman on the phone. The problem was that after five minutes neither of us could understand the other. I politely said goodbye and hung up. I re-dialed hoping I would be rerouted to a U.S. based contact center, which I was. Frustration for the agent and for me as well. Call centers based overseas can often create language problems for customers when the agent speaks with a foreign accent creating frustration on the part of the customer. The above can be technical support centers, information centers or customer service centers.

During my work with various utilities (e.g., Duke Power, Consolidated Edison and many more) as well as with Xerox showed quite remarkably that with each call to the contact center, customer satisfaction and loyalty with that utility or Xerox declined until it reached an unacceptable mediocre level and remained there as customers learned to accept – or rather tolerate less than excellent customer service. Customers make a habit of comparing the service of their utility or Xerox for that matter to the best service they receive from any organization – not just those in your industry.

CUSTOMER SUPPORT

Here are five critical areas that should be considered. Here, customer support relates primarily to areas of emotional support – often softer issues, but critical to the relationship. Recall that a customer has two costs of doing business with your organization: economic and emotional. These five are areas where you have the opportunity to reduce the emotional cost (pain) of the customer:

1. Always being there when the customer needs you. How many organizations today have customers who operate on a 24/7 basis or have locations around the globe? To think that you can support their needs by operating 9-5 Monday through Friday is crazy. One of the worst things that can happen is for the customer to have a crisis and be unable to reach anyone in your organization who can be of support.

2. Being able to resolve problems effectively and efficiently *before* they become complaints. The research conducted by TARP (see Technical Assistance Research Programs in Washington D.C., "Complaint Handling in America") is clear on this point. The longer an issue goes unresolved the harder it is to *ever* satisfy the customer. In fact, there is a threshold in time beyond which no matter what you do or don't do, it won't matter – you have lost the customer – usually for good. Your lack of responsiveness communicates to the customer that *you don't care.* One of the reasons customers decide to do business with an organization is because they strongly believe that if they have any kind of problem, you will be there to assist them. If you don't do that, then they feel they have made a bad choice in doing business with your organization. The research mentioned above also indicates that a problem situation can cause a drop in customer loyalty of as much as 35% or more. The only thing that can offset this is having an expert recovery system in place to preserve the relationship before permanent damage occurs.

3. Ensure your customers and other key stakeholders do not have to learn how your organization works or who they should call in specific situations through the process of trial and error or elimination as this is time consuming and

frustrating – deducting value from the relationship. This includes the concept of single point of contact which over the years more customers, particularly in B2B environments, have told me would be an approach greatly appreciated by them.

4.   Never leaving the customer in a state of uncertainly! People need to know what is being done to rectify a problem, why it occurred and how soon it will be fixed – and to their satisfaction. In the case of a power failure, it is better to be told it will be eight hours and have it come back on in four hours – better to under-promise and over-deliver and not just be told "we're working on it".

5.   One last point here would be *stability of personnel* particularly among the sales force. In interviewing executives of B2B customers over the years they have shown me as many as 25 business cards collected over a three year period from account managers of their key supplier organizations – key account managers who have come and gone. Customers do not enjoy working with strangers. They appreciate having some time to build a good working relationship. If account managers are changing every three months, this is impossible. Just as is it impossible in such a situation to find an account manager who has had the time to really learn about the customer's organization so they can bring suggestions which can help improve the customer's effectiveness or efficiency – not just take an order. This is another cross-over issue involving people, process (sales process), service and support.

TECHNOLOGY

The appropriate use of technology is about selecting and utilizing the latest hardware and software systems capable of enhancing the customer experience. To be successful and add value, technology must not be seen as the end itself – an esoteric pursuit, but rather a means to an end. Organizations need to be mindful of striking the right balance between *hi-tech* and *hi-touch*. How far can you go before losing the customer in the process because it becomes too sterile and impersonal or frustrating and tedious? This is where such approaches as customer labs are very helpful.

Today, most people could pay their bills by internet banking, but there are still those that enjoy human interaction – even as poor as it sometimes may be. Sure everyone could do all their reading on Kindles, but there are some of us that are already tired of looking at anything that even faintly resembles a computer screen, and so, for us the preference is a real book. How well have you identified your customer segments and their unique requirements – appealing to them with an appropriate value proposition? And remember, you cannot be all things to all people. If you attempt this approach you will be doomed to failure. If you have seven consumer segments as Hilton Europe had and you know you can only adequately satisfy four of them, make that your focus unless there is a vital strategic reason not to.

Technology should, above all else, be an enabler. In all the areas of value mentioned above, technology should be appropriately integrated to *add* to the value created and delivered, whether it is integrated into your products, services, support, or helping your people be more successful in their transactions and relationships with customers and other key stakeholders and the list goes on. It must be an enabler and not a detractor from building strong relationships.

There is also the concept of *technology as a service*. As an example, in some organizations around the globe, the responsibility for telecommunications is given to the IT Department – people who are certainly very bright and capable, but know little or nothing about telecommunications. But because senior management sees telecommunications as technology and this department was already engaged in management of technology albeit information technology, they were told to "just get on with it".

So, for example, during my work as Chief Strategy Officer for Cybernet, the largest telecommunication company in Pakistan, we developed diagrams for the IT personnel of key accounts showing all the details of the telecommunications system which Cybernet was operating for their organization. It was done for education purposes and to enhance communication with IT personnel in the customer organization who were less familiar with such systems.

In addition to the example on the facing page, Cybernet also co-developed with the account a 3-year technology roadmap showing how the above diagram would evolve in response to changing business requirements based upon the account's 3-year business plan.

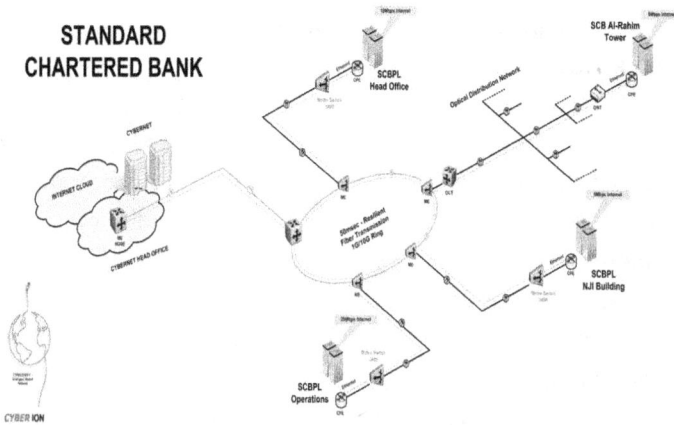

INFORMATION

The challenge here is that most organizations tend to be "data rich and information poor". The prevailing mantra is "if a little data is good, then a lot of data must be even better" or, "whoever dies with the most data wins".

But one key lesson learned here is that, in reality, "data is like sand". This metaphor works well in the Middle East but elsewhere as well. Think about it. If you had a handful of sand, what could you do with it that would be of some value? Throw it in the eyes of a would be attacker I suppose and escape? Fill a small hole? Put it in the sandbox with the rest of the sand for your children to play in with their cars and trucks? However, we know that if sand is subjected to intense heat and a few other ingredients are added, you can create a glass to drink from – now you have something of value! In other words you have, through this transformation process, unlocked the hidden or true value of that sand. So it is with data. Unless you subject it to analysis and interpretation and then report it effectively, review it and act upon it, it is of little value. However, if you follow these steps you transform raw data into actionable information which forms the basis for setting priorities and making effective and efficient decisions. You have, in fact, unlocked the hidden or true value of the data.

An IT department that simply spews out reports filled with data (at the request of senior management who is clueless about the above concept) is, without even realizing it, continuously deducting value from their organization! I had the experience of being asked to assist John Hancock, a large insurance company in the Back Bay area of Boston, and train middle managers – department managers on how to use the reports filled with data that crossed their desks regularly. You see the thing was, at that time, these managers were very busy (at least they said they were – lots of activity, unclear about accomplishment, but nonetheless) and because it took too much time to figure out what these data reports were really saying; or what was important to look for, they just filed them away; or they picked the one or two numbers they thought were most important without having any sound basis for knowing why – it's just what they had always done in that department; or they ignored it altogether and just operated on the basis of gut feel. Is this what you want going on in your organization? The fact is that this practice is going on in far too many organizations today!

For years FedEx had the advantage in the package delivery market because it had an online system that allowed customers to check the status of their delivery at any point. Now this is the accepted standard, but it did give FedEx a competitive advantage because it added value!

Then there are predictive systems. Many telecommunications companies, internet providers and more have the technical capability to identify symptoms which often precede a failure in the system of a key account. By being able to anticipate this and prevent failure of the system and therefore preventing downtime for the client and its customers, adds great value.

Predictive systems have also been used to identify patterns of behavior among customers which often lead to defection. This information enables the organization to perform an intervention to hopefully prevent the customer from leaving them for a competitor. Xerox and Thomson Consumer Electronics used such systems when I consulted to them some time ago.

Faster, more comprehensive, more accurate and timely information – the right information when needed can be powerful – it adds value – internally within your organization or externally with your stakeholders. However, customer feedback information is an indispensable type of management information and can be obtained very simply in most cases. But such information thus gained is many times ignored or never reaches the most senior people in the organization – the senior executives never hearing the true voice of the customer. For example, the simple practice of an executive going down to their contact center, selecting a random sample of agents and then sitting around a table asking questions like: "What are our customers saying? What do they like (about our products, services, support) and what don't they like? What do they say competitors are doing better? Are you seeing any new trends developing or changing requirements?" Do this at least once a month and you and your organization will be better for it!

CUSTOMER ENGAGEMENT

Virtually everything discussed above in terms of sources of value impacts some aspect of the customer engagement with your organization. The aim should be to continually enhance the customer engagement – integrate elements from the eight pillars of service excellence. Make each of the experiences with your customers a memorable one – in a positive sense. In this way customer loyalty and profitability *will* build over time. Again Bain and Company have shown that the longer you are able to keep a customer loyal, the more valuable, economically, they are to your organization. Below is an example in a B2C environment (based on Rautakesko in Finland) and would apply as well to Home Depot or B&Q, IKEA or other retailers where the experiences of a typical customer would be similar to the following:

Managing the Consumer Relationship: Consumer Engagement Map (B2C)

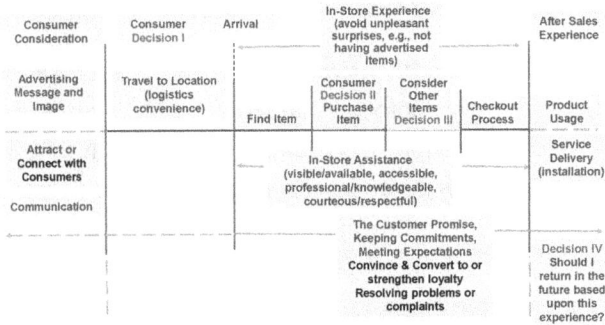

Consumer Consideration	Consumer Decision I	Arrival	In-Store Experience (avoid unpleasant surprises, e.g., not having advertised items)				After Sales Experience
Advertising Message and Image	Travel to Location (logistics convenience)	Find Item	Consumer Decision II Purchase Item	Consider Other Items Decision III	Checkout Process		Product Usage
Attract or Connect with Consumers			In-Store Assistance (visible/available, accessible, professional/knowledgeable, courteous/respectful)				Service Delivery (installation)
Communication							
			The Customer Promise, Keeping Commitments, Meeting Expectations Convince & Convert to or strengthen loyalty Resolving problems or complaints				Decision IV Should I return in the future based upon this experience?

First is the customer consideration stage (should I go or not?) – this is often where the strength of the brand or *pull* of the advertising, the image, the message all come into play.

The customer has four decision points as noted above. As a retailer it is important to know how many of those decisions are made in your favor. Those decisions not only affect your bottom line, but can lead to positive references or negative ones being given to potential customers.

You see that the in-store experience is a blend of your people, the level of service, the products you sell, the checkout experience and, of course, the customer's experience with the product after purchase. There is also the issue of information, technology – literally everything comes into play. If orchestrated properly and if you ensure you are addressing those issues of greatest importance to the customer you can end up a winner! The customer will make purchases, come again and more often while at the same time providing positive references based on their experience. What more could you want?

Most organizations sell multiple products and/or services. Yet too often it is found that customers only purchase one or two of what is available to them. The rest of their needs are met elsewhere by a competitor. The question for management remains, "If we enhance our customer's experiences with us, can we motivate them to purchase possibly three or four of our products and/or services instead of just one or two? What would that be worth?" Getting this right meant millions in added revenue to organizations I worked with such as Irish Life in Dublin, Ireland and Anglo American/Tarmac in the UK.

In closing this chapter, if your organization has a department called *customer service*, what are the other departments supposed to be doing? It was Xerox that once defined a customer focused organization as being one with only two positions. Either you serve the customer directly or you serve someone who is. If you are doing neither, then you serve no purpose in the organization. Something to think about.

Summary Questions for Senior Management Based on this Chapter

Answering the following questions should represent a learning opportunity for you and your MC members regarding Chapter Four:

1. Have you and the leadership team assessed the value being created and/or delivered as a result of (a) your brand strength; (b) your image or reputation as an organization?
    a. What methods have you used to assess it?
    b. What have you learned?
    c. Where and how can you do better — add more value?
    d. How will it help your organization become more competitive or distinguish itself?
    e. Which stakeholder groups recognize the value being created/or delivered?

2. Have you and leadership team assessed the value being created and/or delivered through your processes, in particular the degree to which you

have been successful in (a) making it easy for your stakeholders to do business with your organization (reducing the emotional cost/pain) or (b) being more responsive — reducing cycle time?

a. What methods have you used to assess it?

b. What have you learned?

c. Where and how can you do better — add more value?

d. How will it help your organization become more competitive or distinguish itself?

e. Which stakeholder groups recognize the value being created/or delivered?

3. Have you and the leadership team assessed the value being created and/or delivered through your people? In particular, (a) what capability have you given them to better create or deliver value; (b) what motivation have you given them; (c) what has been the role model behavior by the leadership team you have shown them that encourages them to maximize their value added contribution to relationships between your organization and all the key stakeholder groups?

a. What methods have you used to assess it?

b. What have you learned?

c. Where and how can you do better — add more value?

d. How will it help your organization become more competitive or distinguish itself?

e. Which stakeholder groups recognize the value being created/or delivered?

4. How well have the eight pillars of service excellence been integrated into the daily behaviors and practices of not only frontline people, but those throughout the organization as a way of improving internal as well as external working relationships?

5. Have you and the leadership team assessed the value being created and/or delivered through your products?

a. What methods have you used to assess it?

b. What have you learned?

c. Where and how can you do better — add more value?

d. How will it help your organization become more competitive or distinguish itself?

e. Which stakeholder groups recognize the value being created/or delivered?

6. Have you and the leadership team assessed the value being created and/or delivered through your services and technical support?
   a. What methods have you used to assess it?
   b. What have you learned?
   c. Where and how can you do better — add more value?
   d. How will it help your organization become more competitive or distinguish itself?
   e. Which stakeholder groups recognize the value being created/or delivered?

7. Have you and your leadership team assessed the value being created and/or delivered around the following areas where customers need emotional support: (a) always being there when the customer or stakeholder needs you; (b) resolving problems or complaints effectively and efficiently; and (c) never leaving a customer or other key stakeholder in a state of uncertainty and the others noted above in this Chapter?
   a. What methods have you used to assess it?
   b. What have you learned?
   c. Where and how can you do better — add more value?
   d. How will it help your organization become more competitive or distinguish itself?
   e. Which stakeholder groups recognize the value being created/or delivered?

8. Have you and the leadership team assessed the value being created and/or delivered as a result of the technologies you utilize?
   a. What methods have you used to assess it?
   b. What have you learned?
   c. Where and how can you do better — add more value?
   d. How will it help your organization become more competitive or distinguish itself?
   e. Which stakeholder groups recognize the value being created/or delivered?

9. Have you and your leadership team assessed the value being created and/or delivered through the information you are able to provide to customers or other key stakeholders — providing more comprehensive information, more reliable/accurate information, more relevant/needed information, more accessible information or more timely information?
   a. What methods have you used to assess it?

     b.   What have you learned?

     c.   Where and how can you do better — add more value?

     d.   How will it help your organization become more competitive or distinguish itself?

     e.   Which stakeholder groups recognize the value being created/or delivered?

10. Have you and your leadership team assessed the value being created and/or delivered in the customer or stakeholder experiences — the overall engagement with them in a way that continually improves it and makes them want to do business with your organization even more with each passing day because they consistently see you get the fundamental or routine items done flawlessly and provide *wow* experiences where they count most in strengthening and building long-term relationships?

     a.   What methods have you used to assess it?

     b.   What have you learned?

     c.   Where and how can you do better — add more value?

     d.   How will it help your organization become more competitive or distinguish itself?

     e.   Which stakeholder groups recognize the value being created/or delivered?

11. What is your plan for achieving operational excellence and what progress have you made and how do you know? Where have the stakeholders noticed an improvement? Operational excellence is the foundation upon which value can then be added and recognized so how strong is that foundation?

12. On average, how many products and/or services does a customer have? If you could double that number, what would be the implications to your organization's bottom-line? What actions do you need to take to make that happen in the next 18 months?

13. Have you as CEO and all other members of the MC engaged in a "back to the floor" initiative on a regular basis (quarterly or semi-annual) to assume frontline positions in your organization to listen, learn, engage, build relationships and support the success of your people and customers? How successful has it been? What have you learned and what actions have you taken? Or, what is your plan for pursuing this type of initiative?

As you can see from our model below, the sensing system is where continuous and comprehensive feedback is obtained to understand how your organization is doing – its health, your progress toward the vision, the impact your strategies are having and all the critical pieces of information about your external operating environment that are relevant to your future success and to keeping you on course.

The Sensing System is the focus of this chapter and Chapter Six:

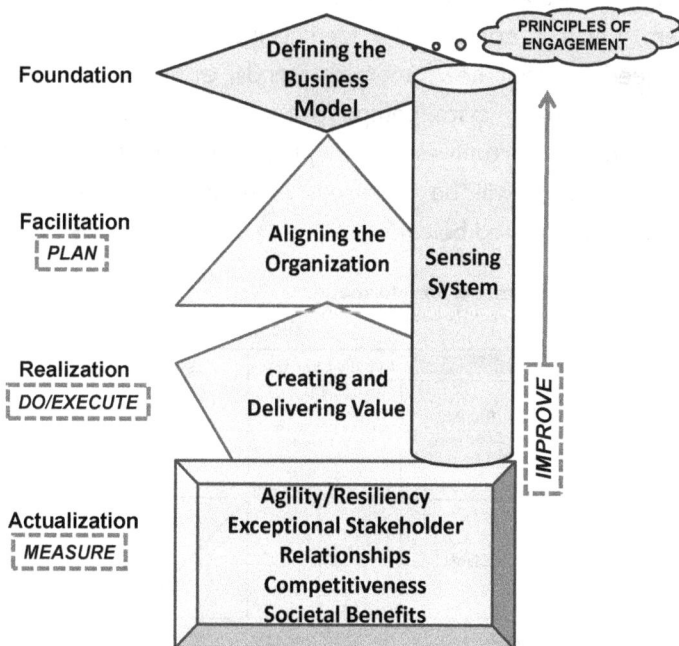

WHISKERS OF A CAT

It may be that many of you readers have had a cat. Even if you have not had one, you are undoubtedly aware of how important the whiskers are to the cat. Suppose your cat woke up tomorrow morning to find its whiskers had mysteriously fallen off during the night! How do you think the cat would behave? Yes, you are right! Probably somewhat erratically – indecisive when it comes to narrow passageways or jumping great heights – clearly more unsure of itself. To sum it up you would be forced to conclude that the cat's judgment was impaired. After all, the whiskers are the cat's primary sensing system to its external environment.

An organization is really no different! Without an integrated, effective, efficient, comprehensive, almost real time sensing system which is continuously feeding intelligence into all those who need it about new emerging trends, evolving technologies, changing consumer taste, competitive actions and other potential threats or opportunities, your judgment and that of your leadership team will be impaired. A simplified picture of the situation is illustrated below:

The changing requirements for information

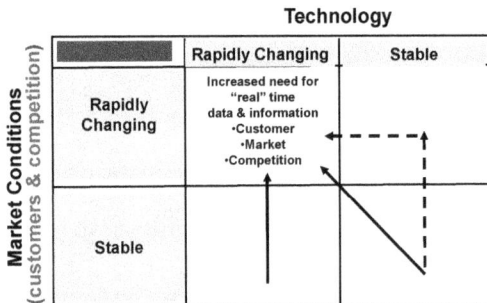

Technology

	Rapidly Changing	Stable
Rapidly Changing	Increased need for "real" time data & information ·Customer ·Market ·Competition	
Stable		

Market Conditions (customers & competition)

Where is your organization today? How fast is your operating and market environment changing?
Whether you like it or not – whether you are ready or not, every organization is moving toward the most uncomfortable cell in the above matrix!

The fact is that you need better and faster information due to the dynamic, turbulent nature of today's business environment. In 1973, when I worked at General Motors, they were in the lower right-hand cell of the above matrix. Their biggest problem was knowing what to do with all the money that was coming in the door. That year, they sold 11.5 million cars and pick-up trucks and had approximately 51% share of the North American market. They were "king of the hill". However, once the Arab Oil Embargo hit in November 1973 and downsizing followed along with more stringent emissions standards, their complacent approach to the market came to an abrupt end. Until then they had been the experts on cars and whatever they decided to build, the public lapped up – like dog food. And it worked because the American public was enamored with large, splashy, powerful, gas guzzling cars. But in a relatively short period of time GM was catapulted into the most uncomfortable box in the above matrix – where everything was changing and the speed of change continued to accelerate. In the meantime, they were not able to adjust their dinosaur management style let alone their draconian culture in order to take the actions that would have enabled them to survive and prosper.

Every organization in the world is moving toward that most uncomfortable box in the above matrix! There are *no* exceptions. The differences are: (1) the speed of movement and (2) the speed with which organizations are able via innovation, adaptation, learning and agility to ensure the needed changes are made and made in a timely manner – all supported by a best practice sensing system. So, my questions are simply these:

> *Where is your organization in the above matrix today? Where will it be tomorrow? How fast are conditions changing in your operating environment and what are you doing to ensure you not only survive but prosper?*

Arnold Glasow – noted American writer and philosopher said, "The only problem with the future is that it is usually here before we are ready for it". Are you ready? Will you be ready? What is your view of the future? Whether you like it or not you are competing for the future – or a place in it and you need to know what it takes to win unless you just want to be second best or worse.

SENSING SYSTEM

Information is the life-blood of any organization. Without it, you are dead in the water. Having too much data and not enough actionable information (the case for this made in Chapter Four) is like the body having too many white cells and not enough red cells. *Information is a strategic asset! It is a key to gaining and maintaining competitive advantage. Having the right information at the right time is indispensable.*

What has been observed in my work around the globe? Aside from there being far too much data and far too little actionable information in most organizations, the IT department including the CIO does not always possess the business acumen needed to contribute to the fullest extent to the success of the organization or to understand where or how to add value. What is needed is a new breed of IT professional.

The leadership team needs to engage in leadership sensing as well. This is of two types. The first is intuitive sensing – just feeling, knowing, without a lot of systematic analysis, the important trends which will shape the future market. Not everyone has this capability – it is a talent more than a skill – being able to see dots others do not see and connect them before anyone else has a clue. This is the passive sensing. Then there is an active sensing. This is a skill which any member of the leadership can gain – and, in fact all should be using. It is simply going out and engaging staff at all levels across the organizations as well as customers and suppliers (the minimum set) on a regular basis to find out what they are seeing and hearing. Then systematically collecting that information on a continuous basis and regularly sharing it with the rest of the leadership team and others in the organization that need to know it. It is surprising how uncomfortable senior executives of many organizations are about doing this! In fact in some organizations, it has **never** been done!

Some Examples

In some of the best organizations such as Proctor and Gamble, Nordstrom's, Lexus, Amazon, Google, Apple, Wells Fargo Bank and others, they have leading-edge information systems, often linked to their strategic intents and internal competencies/strengths. For example, P&G and their market oriented system; Lexus and their customer oriented system; Google, Amazon, 3M and Apple in the innovation oriented system; and so on. Few organizations have it all together – again organizations often tend instead to play to their strengths – the thing or things they believe give them the competitive edge in the market. However, what has been determined in my experience is that if you are going to have a bias the best one to have is probably customer and market focus. Innovation can also be a great one provided you are tapping into the key sources of innovation – namely the customer, your people and suppliers not to mention understanding best practice and competitor behavior.

In 1992, AT&T Universal Card Services in Jacksonville, Florida won the prestigious Malcolm Baldrige Award in Performance Excellence marking it as a world-class organization. One of its strengths was in its customer management practices and processes known as the *Listening Post Team* approach. Today it still remains one of the world's top approaches more than 20 years later!

Monthly meetings were the norm and the team was led by a cross-functional multi-level group including vice presidents and senior vice presidents as well as middle level managers and a host of others. Many of these individuals had responsibility for the various individual listening posts utilized – from complaints, customer satisfaction and loyalty measurement, contact centers and others (see the diagram on the following page). The purpose of the Listening Post Team was to integrate all the streams of customer information and set priorities on the basis of having a complete picture of the customer domain – not just fragments or making decisions on the basis of *islands of information* such as only complaint data. One of the key lessons is *never* to rely on a single source of customer information and always integrate the sources you are using – otherwise sub-optimal decisions from an organizational perspective *will* result – guaranteed.

AT&T Universal Card Services

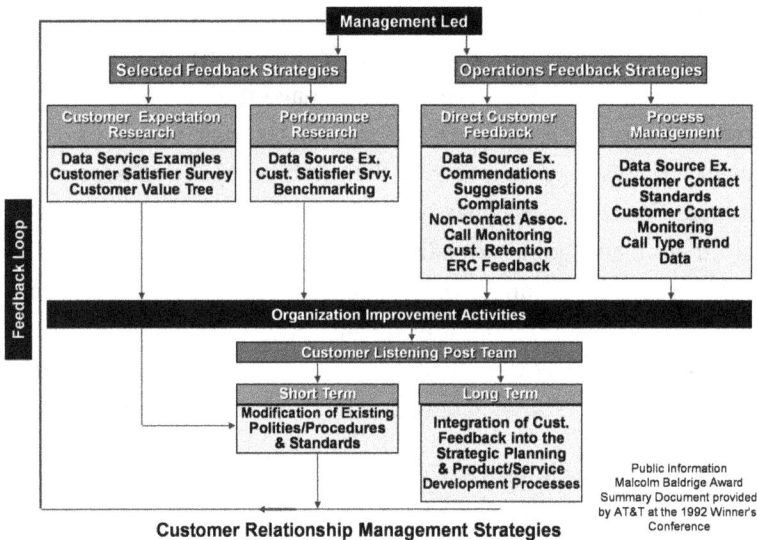

Customer Relationship Management Strategies

For a second example, let's examine the strategic stakeholder architecture shown on the facing page. At the top of this diagram, the *plan* and *do* parts of the Deming cycle, are where your organization's sensing system should be providing you with all the necessary critical data and information you need to then formulate the appropriate stakeholder relationship strategies. The next step is measuring the impact those strategies are having through utilizing various on-going qualitative and quantitative methods (Level 1).

This feedback is then compared with all the other relevant information available for confirmation and to gain deeper or broader understanding of the issues identified through the qualitative and quantitative methods (Level 2). Lastly, priorities are then set, once all the relevant data and information has been integrated so that actions could be taken on behalf of the Listening Post Team established to manage and coordinate all activities related to stakeholder relationships (Level 3). The actions taken by the QITs or SBITs (see diagram for definitions) are monitored regularly by the Listening Post Team to ensure their efficacy or the need for any mid-course corrections.

The Strategic Stakeholder Architecture & Learning System to Drive Change, Innovation & Competitiveness

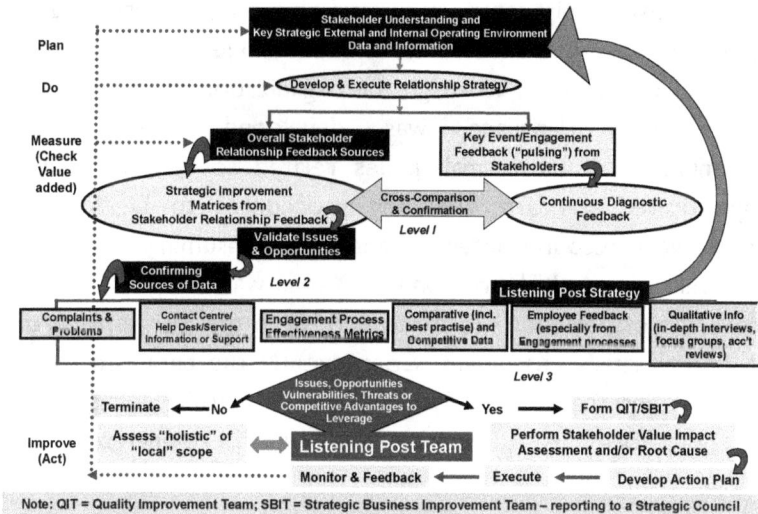

Note: QIT = Quality Improvement Team; SBIT = Strategic Business Improvement Team – reporting to a Strategic Council

The system is strategic in nature. However, the ultimate impact of what is learned or sensed through this system has immediate and significant impact operationally on your organization as well as enhancing its strategic competitiveness. Below are examples from my experiences with Motorola, Asea Brown Boveri (ABB), Xerox, AT&T Universal Card Services and Siemens.

When you are designing and developing a sensing system or strategic information architecture, you basically have two options.

First, create an architecture as in the case of Motorola's ten UPS (universal performance indicators) or the ABB (Asea Brown Boveri) equivalent, both of which focused on internally oriented measures such as operating cost, quality and cycle time and other process effectiveness issues and then work outward – hopefully at some point impacting the customer or end-user in a way that added value. Unfortunately, in my experience, I have seen too many internally focused sensing systems that became an end in themselves as opposed to a means to an end – that end being enhanced competitiveness and customer loyalty through adding value which the customer recognizes and appreciates.

This was a problem for Xerox many years ago with their landmark LTQ (Leadership Through Quality) program – truly one of the most sophisticated, integrated and comprehensive quality systems in the world. However, as I came to learn, it became all-consuming and began to weigh the organization down. In fact, a whole LTQ language was developed internally for communication! Even small issues related to quality required sophisticated standard operating procedures to be followed which were resource intensive and time consuming. Finally, the light bulb went on! The reason that Xerox was doing LTQ was to make the organization more competitive in the marketplace and to better satisfy customers. Consequently the paradigm shifted from an internal quality for the sake of quality focus to an external focus – a healthy one which re-energized the organization.

Allow me to share an example from Siemens Telecommunications U.K. They were a client some years ago. As it turns out, one day I received an urgent call from a senior person in this organization to come and visit because of some serious issues they had. This by the way is the part of the Siemens organization which focuses on installation of telephone systems for hotels, large corporations and such. Upon arrival and meeting with the senior team, it was made clear to me that because of Siemens relentless pursuit of cost reduction (using six-sigma and other approaches) and improvement of operating profit for so many years that the U.K. operation had been emaciated – possibly decimated would be a more apt description. People had been laid off or made redundant leaving a skeleton crew to man the ship and those left behind were now thoroughly demoralized and demotivated. Even more, the customers had witnessed the erosion of service quality and there was a rise in complaints and defections. Senior management told me unequivocally that they thought their organization could persist only about another 18 months and then it would die. Could I help them? The answer was yes, of course and so we embarked on a unique and tailored cultural transformation process which helped to save them and re-energize their people and preserve the relationships with their key customers. So be careful with cost down approaches and their relentless pursuit – they can be extremely damaging!

The better approach in my opinion is to have a sensing system or strategic information architecture driven from the outside in. The example above (as was the case with AT&T Universal Card Services) is such a system, but rather than just focusing on customers alone as in the case of AT&T, the example above focuses on the broad array of stakeholders – of which one is the customer, but also includes many others in the supply (or value) chain as well as business partners, community, regulators and more. Use what you learn to make the internal adjustments needed to meet external stakeholder requirements and expectations. In the end, my observation is that your organization will be more successful and that it will, in fact, come closer to realizing its full potential more quickly.

Notice that the above system, and it is a system composed of multiple systematic, integrated and comprehensive processes, follows the Deming Improvement Cycle: plan; do/execute; measure; improve. These four steps are the basis of any systematic approach and one you should have ingrained in your people at all levels as part of their daily work life. It will make your organization more successful.

Just to recap briefly in simplest terms, these four steps are:

1. **Plan:** Do your homework, gather the right data and analyze it, draw conclusions, involve your people and other stakeholders such as suppliers as needed, establish ownership or accountability, timing, interdependencies, tasks, critical success factors, potential barriers and measures of success as well as the monitoring and communication approach **before** you act!

2. **Execute/do:** Follow the action plan from step one — executing as flawlessly and completely as possible, utilizing the Council concept from Chapter Two and cross-functional teams wherever possible.

3. **Measure:** Assess the impact of your actions. Are they having the desired or expected impact? How do you know? Hopefully you know through the measures of success you specified in the plan step above. You need to know what is changing, where it is changing and how fast it is changing.

4. **Improve:** Based upon the measurement and review of progress, make any mid-course adjustments necessary to stay on track or even enhance impact further — make informed decisions based upon actionable information! Decisions should be fact-based.

So, in the above system, once you have done your planning — collected the right data and information, analyzed it, you can then develop the optimal stakeholder strategies — ones that will allow your organization to build exceptional relationships with all of your key strategic stakeholder groups. On this point, here is a quote from the **U.K. Department of Industry and Trade from 2001**:

> *Only by developing an effective strategy for managing and maintaining excellent relationships with all its key stakeholders can a company hope to achieve its full potential.*

OVERALL STAKEHOLDER RELATIONSHIP FEEDBACK

You need to spend some quality time as a leadership team along with other individuals who have in-depth knowledge of these stakeholder organizations to properly identify them and understand which ones should be considered most important. There should be well defined, well thought out criteria for selection of a most important stakeholder.

In each most strategically important stakeholder organization you should identify at least three possibly more key individuals (generally five maximum). These would be key decision makers, decision influencers, users/user groups to mention just three. They should represent individuals or groups with whom it is vitally important for your people and organization to have an exceptional working relationship.

A quick case in point as to why more than the chief decision maker(s) should be included on your list comes from my many years of work with Boeing/McDonnell-Douglas. It was typical for account managers of Boeing/McDonnell-Douglas, when calling on the Pentagon to sell weapon systems – aircraft in particular, to walk down the long corridor to the General's office, passing numerous Colonels and Lt. Colonels along the way – ignoring each and every one of them even though they were potential decision influencers. Then one day, the account manager arrives and heads to the General's office to find that the General has now retired or moved to another position such as Chief of Staff. Sitting in his place is one of the Colonels that the account manager for years by-passed on the way down the long corridor. Needless to say, the new General and decision maker had little interest in doing business with the Boeing/McDonnell-Douglas organization and precious little time for the Boeing/McDonnell-Douglas account manager!

The other key point here is that if you gather consistent information from at least three to five individuals of a decision making, decision influencing role – or even key users, you can gain as much as 80% of the critical insight you need about that stakeholder organization. A key question that you need to answer for your organization is simply this, "How much information is enough?" While Plato is quoted as saying, "Incomplete information is worthless" probably 80% of the technological advancements in any area of society would fail to exist today if this was the case because the scientists or researchers involved would be afraid to risk moving forward on incomplete information! Yet, we know they had to do so. This is why there are leadership teams who should be capable of making informed decisions, set priorities and allocate resources based on the best available actionable information. Often qualitative rather than quantitative information is richer and more compelling.

For these most strategically important stakeholders, the recommendation is to be "up close and personal" – namely something along the lines of a regular relationship review which consists of four parts: (1) looking to the future; (2) the quality and other key dimensions of the relationship; (3) comparative feedback regarding the best or ideal relationship (gaining competitive intelligence); and (4) more specific performance criteria which you have come to know the stakeholder organization appreciates such as being proactive – these being rated on a 5-point quantitative scale with the account's perception/explanation of any improvement or decline compared to the last performance review. Conducting these quarterly or semi-annually is suggested. Look, the environment is too dynamic, too turbulent to wait for an annual review – by then it is too late. You see that this is the fallacy with key customer accounts. Senior Management believes that the key account manager is taking care of everything – really managing the relationship and keeping the Managing Director informed. Too often, however, the account manager is reluctant to ask the tough questions. Instead he/she simply asks, "How are you doing?" and the expected answer comes back, "OK". He or she them moves on to focusing on getting the order.

Here is an example from Huhtamaki, one of the world's largest makers of disposable products headquartered in Helsinki, Finland. Virtually any plastic or paper cup, for example, used by

McDonalds or found in vending machines would probably be made by Huhtamaki (just check the bottom of the cup or plastic/paper container). I was working with their UK business unit. I had just gone out to conduct the equivalent of a relationship review with seven of their key accounts like Sodexho, a large European catering company. In the course of those discussions I found that several of their most prized accounts were buying all their low end plastic cups by the container load from China. In the meeting with the Managing Director and senior staff to discuss the findings of my qualitative research, I mentioned the situation regarding China. He was absolutely shocked! He could not believe it! No one had told him anything! Needless to say, the air turned a bit bluish afterward. So, I ask, "What are your Key Account Managers **not** telling you and why?"

*Also be aware that the relationship review should **NOT** be done by the account manager!* What has been found is that far too often the key account personnel are reluctant to be completely candid – open and honest in their feedback if the account manager is directly involved. The customer does not want to risk damage to the relationship with the account manager for fear of reprisals (real or imagined) or potentially creating a relationship problem with the account if something negative is said about the account manager. Use of a third party can be beneficial in the sense that an account often views your organization's investment in using a third party objective organization or individual as a positive sign of your commitment to getting and keeping the relationship healthy – namely, you really care. The alternative? Use someone from a part of the organization your key account never deals with such as human resources.

In discussing customers, whether the broader set of B2B customers or your most important consumer segments, you may utilize a quantitative approach where elements of all the customer engagements (similar to either the Xerox Engagement Map or

B2C Engagement Map shown in Chapters Three and Four) are considered in the survey.

Again, it is suggested that for B2C you focus on your most strategically important segments. For example, in working with Hilton Europe I focused attention on a group of customers called Diamond customers. These individuals stay in a Hilton property a minimum of 150 nights per year. While only 5% of the customer base, they represent in excess of 45% of the revenue and profit – pretty significant! So when they say they are unhappy with you, you had better listen and find out why and do so quickly – while tracking their growing or emerging unhappiness so you can avoid a crisis. Unfortunately Hilton Europe did not. However, in this case, solid qualitative research in the form of in-depth focus group sessions of two hours each in at least three locations was imperative to gain the insights from Diamond customers which then were utilized for the broader quantitative survey and formulation of the appropriate strategy.

As you can see from the previous diagram describing the **Strategic Stakeholder Architecture** there is also a pulsing survey underway. These would be done for what your customers consider to be the most important customer experiences (e.g., in the case of Xerox it was repair service). The following approach was done by Xerox Canada.

Across Canada there were approximately 5000 repair service engagements per month. So, each month, two days were selected randomly and each customer having a service repair on the two days selected was sent a short survey (e.g., five to seven questions with sincere lead-in and one open-ended question for additional suggestions or comments as this is often where new emerging or changing requirements are revealed by customers). The response rate was a staggering 65%. Why? Because it was (1) totally relevant – including only those issues which customers through qualitative research had said were important to them; (2) it followed the logic the customer goes through – first a call must be made to the service center to schedule an appointment, then an interaction with a service technician occurs by telephone, then a site visit for the actual repair; and (3) it was what is called a *minimum response burden* to the customer – short, taking about five minutes to complete. Any customer indicating a score of 3 or below on a 5-point scale was contacted to gain further information. This kind of pulsing survey can be utilized with employees, suppliers, virtually any stakeholder group and can be done by telephone, email or even SMS (used by AT&T in America, for example).

There is a new technique called Gavaghi or Sentiment Analysis from the University of Lund in Sweden which allows for the systematic and insightful analysis of any form of communication – written or verbal (recorded conversations with customers such as you might have in your contact center). The point here is that by utilizing this technique, you could simply ask 25% of your employee base (all levels, all functions) one simple question quarterly, "How does it feel to work here" and do it anonymously. The analysis would identify the priority issues without the need for a traditional employee satisfaction survey. Powerful and simple. You would be able to easily identify the holistic issues and the local issues in the case of a global organization. Other questions could be utilized as well.

In terms of contact center recordings, a similar "pulse of the customer" could be maintained to identify emerging trends, likes and dislikes of products, support or services – new as well as existing, competitive intelligence, changing customer requirements and so on.

Teams would exist to analyze and interpret the results from these two different sets of feedback. The information would be cross-compared and priorities identified, but it would not stop there. This was just Level 1 and the start of Level 2.

In level 2 other confirming sources of data and information would be brought into play. For example, it may be that through people feedback, it is found that frontline employees do not feel empowered enough or trained well enough to be able to deal effectively with certain customer issues nor are they supported by IT with the accurate, timely information they need in their CRM system. All of these help pinpoint root causes of any customer problems. Certainly customer complaints would also be included and compared for confirmation and further explanation. The list goes on. As you can see there can be multiple sources of potential confirming data and information which need to be linked up in a strategic customer (or stakeholder) information database. Each stakeholder group would have its own integrated database of joined up data and information sources.

Then, as in the case of AT&T Universal Card Services, there would be a Listening Post Group or equivalent which would look at each stakeholder group, set priorities and determine actions to be taken as well as identify new emerging trends, changing stakeholder requirements and competitive intelligence as appropriate to mention just a few. In the interest of being agile, opportunities would be pursued or threats blunted, regular QIT's (quality improvement teams) or SBITs (strategic business improvement teams) would be formed depending upon whether it was a just a local functional or departmental issue or a holistic (total organization) one, respectively.

The action plan developed would be monitored and measures of success followed to ensure progress was being made fast enough and sufficiently enough to obviate the problem or take advantage of the opportunity. This review would be made to the Listening Post Team (part of the membership being MC members) or other Council depending upon the area, e.g., human performance excellence, operational excellence, relationship mastery or competitiveness and growth and done monthly. Reports would be provided during the regular monthly MC meeting with the CEO/Managing Director.

Feedback to the stakeholders involved would be a regular part of each action plan developed and executed. The worst thing that an organization can do is ask for input from stakeholders and not give them any feedback that their information is being acted upon or letting them know the specific actions being taken and the impact these will have in making them more satisfied in doing business with your organization – or, in the case of your people, more committed to the success of the organization. Again, all actions should be consistent with adding value and being aligned with the purpose and vision of the organization. Behaviors and practices in conjunction with execution of actions would be monitored as well to ensure alignment with the organization's values/beliefs.

You now have a picture of how a strategic information system or sensing system could be structured. Every organization would have a different one – again possibly biased toward its strengths whether competitive in nature, innovation focused, people oriented or simply holistic. In any case, it should be designed to dramatically enhance (take to the next level) an organization's *Decision Intelligence – it's capability to make optimal strategic and operational decisions at hyper-speed*. That process needs to possess certain characteristics as shown in the diagram on the next page.

As you can see, the process must first be systematic, integrated and comprehensive. The steps must be well-defined and flow from planning and decision-making to execution. Then there must be methods – measures or indicators by which we can assess the impact our decision is having, whether the desired impact or some unintended consequences. We must also ensure that we learn from what we have done and how we have done it so that the next time we will be better and faster than before. That learning should allow us to innovate by asking what can we do better or differently next time?

The Decision Making Process High Level View

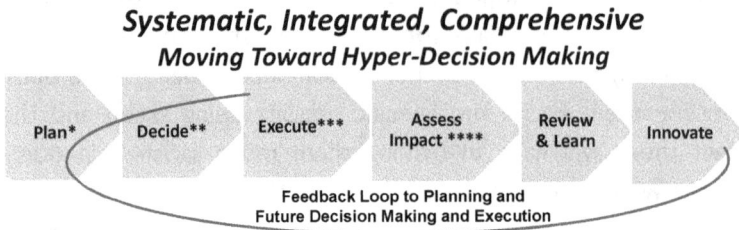

Systematic, Integrated, Comprehensive
Moving Toward Hyper-Decision Making

Plan* ▶ Decide** ▶ Execute*** ▶ Assess Impact **** ▶ Review & Learn ▶ Innovate

Feedback Loop to Planning and
Future Decision Making and Execution

* = Identify, collect and analyze the right and most comprehensive data and information; ensure that not only core decision factors but also other 'influencing' factors are considered; include a rigorous evaluation (not just a 'gut feel') of the potential consequences of alternatives including what would happen if only 50% of the desired impact occurred; the value created and/or delivered and to whom; what if we did nothing!

** = Is the decision approaching optimality?
*** = Is the execution flawless?
**** = Are the right, best and most advanced analytical tools being utilized for assessment?

An optimal decision would be defined as meeting #1 and then at least four of the remaining seven conditions:

1. It either *creates or delivers value* or both to ensure key stakeholders receive benefit
2. Execution is flawless and complete to ensure the desired and/or maximum impact
3. It is in alignment with or consistent with the organization's purpose and vision
4. All behaviors and practices in which the organization engages throughout the formulation and implementation of the decision must be consistent with the beliefs/values of the organization
5. It must contribute to enhancing the competitiveness of the organization
6. It reflects the organization's agility and/or resiliency
7. The cost of lost opportunity is minimized (e.g., factors such as speed of decision, having a systematic process, making a sub-optimal decision or having poor execution can all reduce the impact which a decision may have)
8. It is the right decision for the business — one which better ensures its long-term sustainability

The cost of lost opportunity and how it can work against you

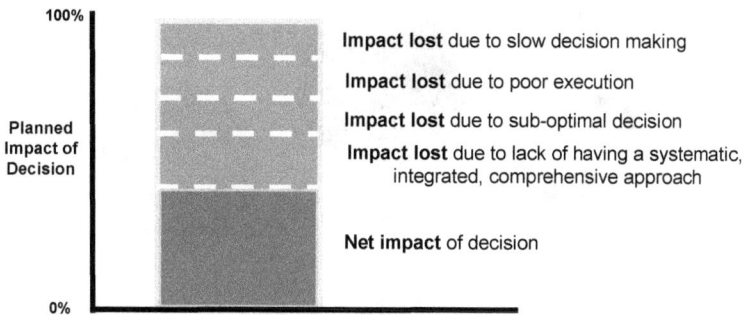

A challenge for any organization would be to make decisions which produce the greatest value for the most stakeholders in the shortest time and with the least investment. Such decisions would, by definition, enhance competitiveness as value is the great differentiator in the market. Knowing your organization's decision intelligence quotient can be important to reaching its full potential and avoiding a significant cost of lost opportunity.

In addition, one needs to be clear regarding the factors that influence decision making in an organization and, therefore, its decision intelligence quotient. In my experience, I have identified the following eight factors which can influence how decisions are made in an organization. For example if your people do not have the capability they need or think they need, they will be overly cautious, risk averse. Or if you have a blame culture where management plays the role of sheriff always looking to catch someone doing something wrong, then decision making will be slower as decisions will invariably be pushed to the top of the organization and not made at the level they should be.

In Chapters Six and Seven we will begin a discussion regarding the holistic performance measurement categories which should be utilized as well as those which in the future should form the basis of a new generation balanced scorecard of performance for organizations.

The critical success factors behind effective decision making

Some valuable resources to be aware of are (1) Quantellia and the World-Modeler technique - the thought leading organization (which is supporting Project OMEGA) in Decision Intelligence and partner of Informed Decisions, Sweden; (2) Ontonix in Switzerland which deals with complexity issues and big data; (3) University of Lund and their Gavaghi technique; (4) the book "Enterprise Architecture Made Simple" from Informed Decisions.

SUMMARY QUESTIONS FOR SENIOR MANAGEMENT BASED ON THIS CHAPTER

Answering the following questions should represent a learning opportunity for you and your MC members regarding Chapter Five:

1. Looking at the matrix in this chapter titled *Changing Requirements for Organizational Information*, where was your organization three years ago? Where is it now? How will the situation be even more challenging in the next 18 months to three years?
    a. How difficult will it be for you to address the challenges you see coming?
    b. What actions will you take to address the challenges you see coming?

2. If you and the MC had to describe the sensing system through which your organization gains critical insight into its operating environment and assesses its own health and competitiveness, how would you describe it? Here is a challenge. On a flip chart, break your MC into teams of four to six. Each team will draw a picture of how it sees your organization's sensing system. Include words to help convey feelings and important ideas which can more clearly communicate to others how your team sees the sensing system. Share and compare, discuss, identify opportunities for improvement/vulnerabilities — areas where you may have a blind spot or insufficient information to allow optimal decisions or to identify, assess and act on opportunities or address threats fast enough.
    a. What are the strengths of your current sensing system?
    b. What does each team believe is the number one most important improvement that needs to be made to better ensure agility, resiliency, adaptability, innovation, customer & market focus, futures orientation, learning or other factors critical to your organization's success, profitable growth and competitiveness?

3. How would the MC define *optimal* decision in your organization? Is it one which is effective and efficient? Adds value? Ensures alignment with the vision, purpose and principles of engagement? Does it reflect consistency with values/beliefs? What is your record of making optimal decisions?

4. How would you rate your organization's decision intelligence on a scale of 1-5 where 1=poor and 5=excellent? What were the reasons for your score? If it was less than a '5' also indicate what you believe needs to be done to move it to a '5'.

5. What is the worst decision you and the leadership team have made for the organization as a whole in the past 18-24 months? What was the

cost of making this decision ultimately (include any cost of lost opportunity)? What can you do to prevent a reoccurrence of this type situation?

6. What do you and the leadership team consider to be the best decision you have made for your organization in the past 18-24 months? What makes it best? How have you assessed the impact of that decision – what measures tell you it was right for the organization?

7. What is the number one improvement you need to make in order to ensure faster decision making?

8. What is the number one improvement you and the leadership team believe needs to be made to make consistently higher quality, more optimal decisions?

9. If you had each member of the MC list the data/information/KPIs they depend upon most for (1) understanding the health of their part of the business for which they are accountable and (2) for making the best decisions, what would they say? What would be different? What would be similar? How should that influence the measures you, as a leadership team, monitor going forward?

10. Peter Drucker has said that "leadership is much more about *doing the right things for the business* rather than doing things right". What does that mean to you and your leadership team? What does it say about how you should make decisions and what decisions should be made?

11. What is the level of integration of your information systems on a scale of 1-5 where 1=poor, 2=fair, 3=good, 4=very good and 5=excellent? Or are you still using what might be termed an *islands of information* approach – fragmented, disconnected? How can you improve the situation and why would it make sense to do so, i.e., what would be the benefit to the organization and the leadership team?

12. What do you and the leadership team believe is the strongest component of your current sensing system? Is it the customer component? The process component? The people component? The technology/innovation component? The financial component? Other?
    a. What makes it your strongest component? What do you do in this sensing area that you do not do in others?

b. Why is the data and information coming through this sensing area of greater value to you?

c. How do you use this data and information to help achieve competitive advantage?

d. What are the one to two opportunities for further improvement of this component?

e. What other components could be added or strengthened to provide better insight, be more holistic, be more proactive through cross-comparison or use of analytical techniques?

f. What is the value that would be added by doing so — for your organization? For you as the leadership team?

13. What are the key strategic positions in your organization (e.g., the most critical positions)? What process did you use to identify them? How effective are the people in those positions at making optimal decisions? Do they have the capability they need to make optimal decisions regularly? What is it costing you in terms of lost opportunity if they aren't? How do you get better?

14. How do you continuously guard against collecting data for data's sake — that is, taking the approach that "if a little data is good, then a lot of data is better"? Who should have ownership for this and how can you all support that person or persons? How do you ensure that the necessary resources are being dedicated to the analysis of that data using the latest and most advanced techniques to unlock the information value of the data and turn it into the actionable information you need for timely and effective (or optimal) decisions made at hyper-speed?

Chapter Six

Leveraging Your Sensing System, Part II

We now come to what I refer to as the *actualization* stage. This is where everything that your organization has done as a direct consequence of your leadership comes together and either sets the standard by which others are compared or marks you as an *also ran* or mediocre organization.

In today's world, what are the results which can really distinguish your organization from the rest of the pack? If I had to pick just a few, they would be the following:

- Competitiveness
- Exceptional stakeholder relationships
- Agility/resiliency
- Societal benefits (such as sustainability)

Each of these will be discussed briefly in Chapter Seven along with the other critical outcomes you should be aiming for as an organization – a new generation balanced scorecard in effect. However, as you may already understand, these outcomes or results are not independent of each other. There are inter-relationships, inter-dependencies. They form part of a total organization performance measurement and management architecture. Nevertheless, in terms of trying to maintain organizational focus, it is useful to view them as discrete issues, but also be aware of their linkages. For example, you know that by being more agile, your organization should become more competitive. Competitiveness could be considered the dependent variable and agility the independent variable. But in real life, there is a tendency to create strategies and take actions which build the strength of each of these independently while at the same time having an awareness and appreciation for their connectedness.

BALANCED SCORECARD — IN THE BEGINNING...

I always found, when working with organizations, that asking the leadership team of an organization the following question could tell me a great deal about them (e.g., the quality or effectiveness of the leadership team) as well as the organization, "When you are all together, what do you spend your time talking about?" One thing that can be said and this has been confirmed over and over again through research around the globe with organizations (including my own research and client experiences) is simply that the leadership team of the vast majority of organizations spends less than 5% of their time on anything remotely related to strategic or futures oriented issues (where futures oriented means looking beyond quarterly earnings per share). That is roughly one day per month *maximum* on strategic issues.

In these discussions with the leadership team it was not uncommon for them to indicate that they spent as much as 50% to 80% of their time on financially related matters. The rest of their time? Well maybe 15% on process related issues – although they were really not process issues per se. They were much more activity based issues like how many widgets got produced or shipped last month or how many orders did we get in.

The remaining 5%? Often, but not always, was split between customers and people. The customer usually comes up in the discussion when there is a crisis with a key account or consumer defections are becoming rampant.

Or it may be that the results of an employee satisfaction survey just came back and it showed that employees do not trust management! Too often senior management are heard to say, "We can't share this with employees! We have to bury it."

A common response to product or service problems is for senior management to say, "What's wrong with our profitability in Product X or Service Y? Get going – we need to fix it!" So everyone scurries off and tries to fix it. However, it is often the case that no one, including senior management understands what *it* is! Part of the reason being that no one really understands the business processes and other critical factors (*drivers*) that determine profitability of Product X or Service Y and so do not have the right data, information and analysis to pinpoint the issue or it may be that they are being misled by utilizing the wrong KPIs.

But what about the balanced scorecard? The balanced scorecard concept came into being in 1987. In fact, in 1987 it was free for the asking. It was part of the original draft of the Malcolm Baldrige Performance Excellence Criteria. At that time, I was invited to Washington D.C. as one of a group of 40 experts from around America to do a review and comment on the draft award criteria! Then in 1988 it was launched formally – with Motorola becoming one of the first winners that year based to a large extent on their six-sigma efforts. In 1992, the European Foundation for Quality Management Business Excellence Award criteria was launched and those too had a balanced scorecard measurement approach – although one of their measurement components focused on societal benefits whereas Baldrige did not.

As mentioned earlier, Motorola had their ten UPS measures and ABB (Asea Brown Boveri) a similar approach with a larger number of measures – all internally related to quality, cycle time and cost for the most part. They then tried to drive from these indicators of performance to achieve greater external success – trying to dramatically drive down defects to a six-sigma level or 3.4 defects per million opportunities. Motorola was successful. ABB was not. However, as you may know, it was, in the end, only a mediocre success as neither of these organizations has really stood the test of time and set the standard by which others are compared.

Just as an aside, I remember sitting in one of Motorola's Global Quality Reviews in Wiesbaden, Germany some years ago. The Japanese business unit was reviewing their ten UPS measures. When they had finished, I raised my hand and asked, "What about the customers? Have you observed any increase in customer satisfaction or loyalty or increase in positive referrals or sales as a result of your efforts?" They said, "What a good question", but they did not have the answer! Don't find yourself in the same situation. The objective of *any* internal improvement efforts should be to create and add value to some key stakeholder group particularly your customers and thus end up doing a better job of satisfying them and increasing their loyalty.

The other key learning over time has been that the best sensing systems are a good balance of qualitative and quantitative information. Unfortunately, what has been seen too often is a decided bias toward capture and use of quantitative information – survey based data in particular. My experience is that such data provides only a starting point for finding out what is really going on – it is a way of scanning the horizon to see what might be there – much as a sea captain might have had a sailor in the proverbial bird's nest of a ship in the 17th century with a telescope watching for approaching land or other vessels. Often when you do a deep dive beneath the surface of the quantitative data through focus groups or in-depth interviews, you find that the *problem* is often *not* the *problem*! It is something else entirely. The survey question was merely acting at best as a mediocre surrogate for the real issue.

Qualitative information is much more rigorous and rich in detail. Spending an hour in an in-depth interview with an executive or a two hour focus group with ten frontline employees yields tremendous information. And, the fact of the matter is that conducting three focus groups, for example with employees or customers in different locations and in homogeneous peer groups can provide up to 80% of the information you need in virtually any situation. If you have need for more information, by all means construct your broader quantitative surveys based upon your qualitative findings. But I warn you, you may still need to do a little digging at the end of it all to ensure you have arrived at the right conclusions – not as much, but some.

Xerox was the "king of the quantitative methodologies". Their capstone was their global core group approach whereby they attempted to standardize the questions in their customer surveys globally – at least up to a point. In other words, each country was required to include certain questions or measures on their customer surveys. Some small number of other questions could be added to cover local conditions. They were constantly looking at how they could move the needle on customer satisfaction so to speak. In fact, the reward structure was such that unless management achieved a customer satisfaction score above a certain threshold, they did not gain access to the larger bonus pool. The result was, in many cases, people taking actions (unnatural or not!) designed to *move the needle* rather than to move the company forward. The other point they missed was, based upon research I conducted while part of Walker: Csm in Indianapolis, Indiana was that in some cultures a rating of a '5' is never given. In other cultures, a '4' is really considered the equivalent of a '5'. The consequence of this was that even though the same questions were asked, direct comparisons were relatively meaningless on a global basis without appropriate adjustments.

The other critical issue here is that customer satisfaction is only table stakes – it allows you to continue to be in the game. However, as referenced previously, customer satisfaction ≠ customer loyalty. **Customer satisfaction + value = customer loyalty.** You can think of customer satisfaction as a measure of *how well your organization played the game* and customer loyalty as *whether your organization won or lost.*

There are two further points which you might want to include in your thinking: (1) never use four point scales as the results will be positively biased and not give you a true picture; and (2) the best measure of customer loyalty is *willingness to recommend*. Here is where Xerox *missed the boat* unfortunately – too much focus on customer satisfaction (just requirements, performance against requirements and relative importance of requirements) and too little attention to customer loyalty (e.g., bringing value into the equation). See the Harvard Business Review article by Jones and Sasser, "Why Satisfied Customers Defect" for more information on this point.

In another situation, General Motors dealerships would regularly invite customers to come in so that the dealership personnel could help customers fill out the customer satisfaction surveys they had received on service and delivery to better guarantee higher scores and better incentives from home office to the dealership. Move that needle!

The traditional balanced scorecard looks something like that pictured below:

Balanced Scorecard (of KPI's)

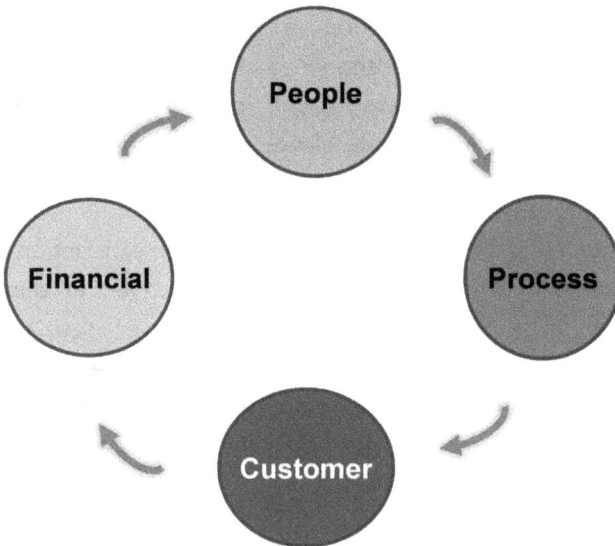

There is good logic to this approach, but it has severe limitations as will be discussed below. So, if your internal and external sensing system is not providing feedback in at least these four areas on a continuous, timely and accurate basis, then you've got a problem – or soon will have. Of course, the leadership team too often operates on the basis of filtered information – information that on its way up to senior management in report formats is sterilized to remove the truth about what is really going on – the true voice of the customer, the employees, the process or even the financials.

The logic in this diagram is inescapable and simply this. *All business results are the consequence of people working in a process.* It just does not happen any other way. If either of those two or both are dysfunctional, then you *will* encounter performance problems. Would you rather have great people and dysfunctional processes or the reverse? The correct answer is, simply, "people make the difference". Great people will perform heroic efforts, work around dysfunctional processes to get the job done and take care of the customer every time. I've seen it over and over again. Simply empower your people to fix the processes as they will know best what to do!

On the other hand, if done right, your people and your process together can act as twin turbo-chargers on your organization's engine to achieve significantly higher levels of performance. The other bonus here is that if you design, develop and improve in these areas of people and process you will gain a lasting competitive advantage which competition will be unable to copy. On top of this, if you fuel the engine with the right stakeholder feedback – both qualitative and quantitative, it is like using 98 Octane petrol. It will drive your improvements in a way that will add value in your relationships with those key stakeholders and further strengthen your competitive advantage – nirvana!

In 1987 I was part of a Core Team that was responsible for a customer focused cultural change effort at Xerox Canada. Dave

McCamus, then the President of Xerox Canada launched the first meeting of the Core Team. He started by drawing the following chart on a flip chart:

The Leap of Faith

Customer Satisfaction ⟷ Employee Satisfaction ⟹ Shareholder Satisfaction

Dave's philosophy in leading Xerox Canada was simply, "If we take care of our customers and employees that will lead us to the financial results we want most." It was a longer-term view – not the usual short-term "give me better quarterly earnings per share (EPS)", but it was what Dave believed was doing the right thing for the business – the essence of what Peter Drucker considers true leadership. Dave had many confrontations with Xerox HQ U.S. in Rochester, New York over this, but he stood firm. Within 18 months or less, Canadian results started to show a sharp improvement and not long after, teams of people from Xerox HQ came by plane or car to Toronto, Canada to find out what their Canadian operation was doing differently and better!

If you get the people and process right, however, especially those depicted in earlier examples of the Customer Engagement Map and the various customer experiences that take place by the hundreds every day between your organization and its people, processes and customers, then the customers will be better cared for – relationships of better quality will be built and regularly reinforced. Value will be perceived and appreciated by the customer. Loyalty will increase and your revenue and profitability as an organization will improve. For evidence to support this conclusion refer to "The Loyalty Effect" by Fred Reichheld, "The Service–Profit Chain" by Heskett et al and "Why Satisfied Customers Defect" by Jones and Sasser.

There are a couple of key places where things can go wrong. The first is that too often the KPIs (Key Performance Indicators) tend to be corporate level or mega measures like market share or profitability or EBIT (earnings before interest and taxes also sometimes referred to as operating profit) and so on. The fact of the matter is that these indicators tend to be at such a high level and influenced by so many other variables that they themselves tend to be relatively insensitive to changes that are going on internally or externally in your organization's operating environment – they tend to mask the real changes.

The second issue is that the KPIs are not always linked up to the critical success factors (4 CSFs shown in the diagram below) of the organization and not linked to the drivers (10 shown in the diagram below) of those CSFs or linked to the KBOs related to the drivers. Often they are just the generally accepted measures – the ones that have always been used or are easiest to measure. Consequently what is needed is the approach mentioned in Chapter Two on Alignment.

Vision Alignment

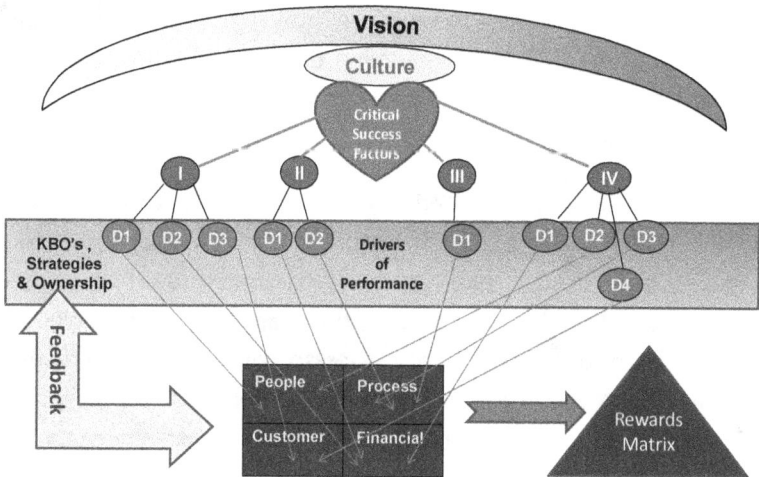

This diagram attempts to capture in a comprehensive manner the vision alignment process. This process will be described in further detail in a Chapter in Volume II. However, as you can see, from the vision, we identify the critical success factors that will enable us to achieve the vision. At the next level down we look at the drivers of performance for each of those critical success factors. In other words, what will ultimately determine the level of performance or excellence we can or will achieve in each of those critical factors? From those drivers, we then establish key business objectives and then the strategies that will allow us to achieve them. We must also identify ownership for achieving those key business objectives and establish measures of success for each key business objective that we can monitor to determine if we are making progress or not, where and how fast. The rewards matrix as described in Chapter Two is the one which links attainment of targets or key business objectives with behaviors aligned or consistent with the organization's values/beliefs.

Just remember, the Titanic *sank* not because of what the Captain or navigator saw, but because of what they did not see! 90% of an iceberg's mass is under the water where it cannot be seen. It is the same as your measurement system – your sensing system. If it is only picking up the top 10% with your corporate level measures and you are missing the 90% that really make the difference – the 90% that determine the level of performance in those 10% you look at, then you too might be headed for an unpleasant surprise.

That is why care is exercised in the above model to ensure the symptoms are seen before it becomes a terminal disease! You need to be proactive, **not** reactive – to anticipate where things are headed, why they are heading there and how fast as well as being able to identify the root causes so you can take corrective actions to prevent reoccurrence. For example, trying to utilize numbers from your CFO is often like looking into the rearview mirror of your car rather than looking through your windshield at what is coming – it speaks to the past, not the future. The same is true for big data. Remember Steve Jobs is quoted as saying "Big data is about the past. Decisions are about the future."

SOME POTENTIAL TRAPS TO WATCH OUT FOR

Just two more points based upon experience. One of these again from Xerox and the other from one of the largest paper products companies in the world based in Helsinki, Finland called StoraEnso.

In the first case, Xerox would survey their customers to determine their satisfaction levels compared to competitors in a range of product and service areas (e.g., ease of use, availability of supplies, cost of supplies, scheduling service calls to the customer site and so on). That was good. However, because of the desire to be the best in all areas, what would happen was that if the Xerox satisfaction score fell below a competitors in any area, Xerox management would immediately want to improve their approach and beat competition in that particular area. On the surface it sounds like a sensible course of action if you want to be the best. However, one day in a management meeting to review the latest comparative customer satisfaction results, senior management was about to launch several time consuming, resource intensive improvements designed to beat the competition in a few areas of performance. I suggested to senior management that they consider the following before moving further: "Are the areas in which improvement was being sought important to the customer or not?" They did not know. But in finding out the answer, they came to realize that these issues were far down the customer's priority list. So, "Why not let competition continue to invest unnecessarily to be the best in those areas since, in reality they are wasting their money as it is not important to customers?" In the end, management agreed with the logic.

During my activity with StoraEnso they conducted a comparative customer satisfaction survey covering all the key dimensions of paper quality, availability, pricing and so on. However, their situation was a little different. One of the key questions on the StoraEnso survey was "How do you, the customer, view

StoraEnso compared to the competitors?" The answer to this question was that the vast majority of customers viewed StoraEnso "just the same as the competitors" – in other words, the customer could not tell the difference – all their suppliers including StoraEnso looked the same to the customer. In effect the customer was saying it really does not matter which company we do business with because they are all the same. What this clearly implied was that StoraEnso was doing nothing to distinguish itself in the mind of its customers! No differentiation based on value and therefore the basis of competitiveness was lost to them. They thought their customers were interested only in cost and availability. Don't let this myopic view exist in your organization!

In the next Chapter I will provide my view on what the next generation of balanced scorecard might look like – or at least, the categories of key performance indicators which organizations should consider as they compete for the future and ask what it takes to win. Frankly, if the measurement categories which will be described are not yet on your radar screen, you should consider increasing the range of your radar to now include them.

SUMMARY QUESTIONS FOR SENIOR MANAGEMENT BASED ON THIS CHAPTER

Answering the following questions should represent a learning opportunity for you and your MC members regarding Chapter Six:

I. When you and the MC get together at your monthly review meetings, what do you talk about? What percentage of your time is taken up in discussions around these topics?
    a. People/human performance excellence
    b. Customers and other key stakeholders
    c. Process (not just activity!)/operational excellence
    d. Financials (traditional and nontraditional – *nontraditional* would include such items as the financial benefits of increasing customer

retention by 10% or reducing complaints by 20% or generating 10% more positive references from existing customers)
e. Strategy/futures oriented topics
f. Leadership and Organizational capability
g. Competitiveness and profitable growth
  i. What can each of you do better or differently as a member of the leadership team to be more effective, help your organization be more competitive or grow more profitably?
  ii. How can you improve your teamwork as the leadership team so you are an example to your people?
  iii. What are some innovative approaches you can utilize to better ensure profitable growth over the next three years?
  iv. What can you do better or differently starting tomorrow to improve your organization's performance and make it more competitive?
h. How balanced is your time between these critical issues 'a' through 'g' above, between operational and strategic? What should you do differently? What steps can you take to make that happen?
i. Are you and your actions aligned with your organization's purpose and vision?

2. Identify the three to five financial results or outcomes you and the leadership team want most. For each one, identify three to five factors that influence or determine the level of performance in each of them. Do you have submeasures/lower level measures (drivers of performance) for each of these factors which you monitor regularly?

3. Have each member of the leadership team identify the two to three (maximum of five) indicators/measures/KPIs that they rely on most to tell them the health of the organization (or the part of it for which they are accountable) in each of the following areas, and arrive at a common set of indicators/measures/KPIs which everyone can use:
a. People (human performance excellence)
b. Process (operational excellence)
c. Customer/key stakeholder groups (relationship excellence/mastery)
d. Innovation
e. Financial
f. Competitiveness and profitable growth
g. Societal

4. Have each member of the leadership team define leadership effectiveness and compare definitions. Agree on one definition, then discuss what indicators/measures/KPIs are that can be established to monitor it. How should you measure that behaviors and practices, consistent with your organization's values and beliefs, are being used throughout the organization as well as by each member of the leadership team?

5. Have each member of the leadership team rate the leadership team on a scale of 1-5 where 1=poor, 2=fair, 3=good, 4=very good and 5=excellent for the following:
   a. Making operational decisions
   b. Making strategic decisions

6. What percentage of time does each leadership team member spend addressing problems or opportunities in a fire-fighting mode or crisis mode? Following a systematic approach: plan, do/execute, measure, improve?

7. What percentage of decisions are made in isolation by a single member of the leadership team and what percentage are made by involving other staff members at different levels and even different functional or business areas of the organization to ensure a more optimal decision? That is, to what degree does each leadership team member take a participative approach to decision making or a lone wolf, go-it-alone approach?

8. What can be done to improve the effectiveness and efficiency of decision making, priority setting and resource allocation at the leadership level? At all levels? How could the concept of Councils discussed in Chapter Two be applied?

9. How does the leadership team define optimal decision? What percentage of decisions made by the leadership team are optimal? What about at other levels in the organization? How could you assess your cost of lost opportunity? How can this be improved?

Chapter Seven

Looking to the Future

In this author's mind, the traditional elements of the balanced scorecard, while effective in their time, are insufficient in today's business environment if an organization is serious about wanting to achieve sustained competitive advantage.

Actualization activities are the focus of this chapter:

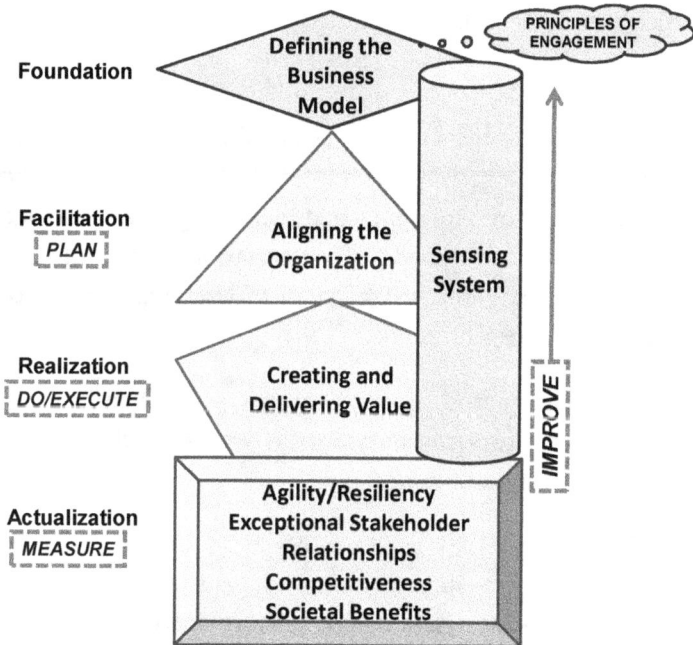

I am **not** saying that every organization should utilize all of the measurement categories suggested in this chapter. However, every organization should review them and consider what is most appropriate in their context – their markets, technologies, customers, competitors — the operating conditions and organizational context. Possibly some would not be utilized at all at the present time. In other cases derivatives or drivers of some of these might be utilized. The original balanced scorecard discussed in Chapter Six is a great foundation for any organization and if you are not yet at that point, start there by all means. However, your measurement system must evolve to meet changing organizational needs and the dynamics of the operating environment. While you should play to your strengths as discussed in Chapter Five regarding sensing systems, you must also gain the discipline and perspective that enables you to see the need for a more balanced and comprehensive performance measurement approach in the future.

NEXT GENERATION OF THE BALANCED SCORECARD

Based upon years of experience and identifying how performance measurement and the needs of organizations are evolving, the following, in my opinion, will become of vital importance to the future success of organizations.

Below is an integrated, comprehensive set of qualitative and quantitative indicators and measures as well as both internal and external results and outcomes.

Let's take a quick look at each of these broad performance categories. Clearly every organization must define what the specifics are in terms of the unique performance measures within each of these broader performance categories. Rather than going into detail at this point, the discussion will include a few key explanatory notes regarding the elements of this new generation balanced scorecard. The specific key performance indicators will be a focus of the next volume in this series.

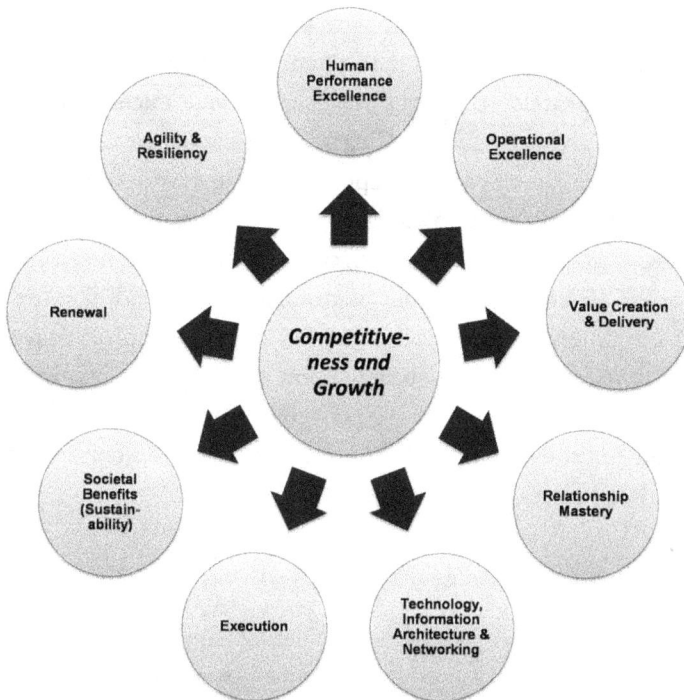

OPERATIONAL EXCELLENCE (OE)

Call it the relentless pursuit of excellence – always looking for ways to reduce variability and therefore improve consistency, getting closer to six-sigma quality in those areas which are critical to the customer and other key strategic stakeholder groups.

Every aspect of the Xerox or the B2C (Rautakesko) engagement map whether installation, training, in-store assistance, the checkout process with the cashier or others must have operational excellence as its foundation – a foundation on which value can then be added in a way that customers recognize and appreciate – reliability, being routinely flawless on the basics must be the foundation. This is especially the case with those experiences which the customer views as most important such as repair service in the case of Xerox copier customers.

Keeping it simple, easy, uncomplicated, fast and enjoyable with **no** unpleasant surprises. Ensuring the people in your organization are putting into practice the eight pillars of service excellence can be the keys to greater success. Clearly, operational excellence must cover product, service and support. There is no question that lean six-sigma can be a valuable approach for most organizations. However, as with the LTQ approach of Xerox, it must not be viewed as an end in itself, but as a means to an end. It must not focus on simply reducing cost, but on creating and/or delivering value. In most cases, and based upon my experiences, either a Green Belt or Yellow Belt selectively chosen and supported is sufficient for the vast majority of process improvement and other value adding activities based upon lean six-sigma.

HUMAN PERFORMANCE EXCELLENCE (HPE)

If you are really serious about releasing the potential of your people, it is necessary to move beyond a focus on just the basic three: obedience, diligence and expertise. These alone identify your organization as being managed – not led and as an organization which will have a tendency toward command and control – not empowerment.

Those characteristics which represent the profile of people in a top tier organization, one which is focused on human performance excellence not just people/personnel management, would include:

- People who take the initiative (e.g., no fear, encouragement to take risks, no blame, learn from mistakes, try a lot of things and see what works, motivated, committed);

- People who are creative because they feel and, in fact, are empowered, have a sense of ownership, pride and are switched on by being able to contribute to the future success of the organization. They possess the capability to make a valuable contribution to the future success of the organization because leadership invests in them so they reach their full potential to contribute. Senior management sees their role, in part, as identifying and eliminating any barriers which could prevent that contribution from being made and doing so as quickly as possible – listening and learning, engaging employees and acting on their feedback/inputs. The people of the organization are involved – participating in creating the future for the organization.

- The HR function must focus on strategic issues and contribute at that level, not just be focused on administrative personnel related issues if it is to add true value in achieving greater organizational success.

- People who are passionate – leadership having reached into not only their minds but their hearts to increase the emotional attachment each and every employee has for that organization, the level of teamwork (all one team) therefore ensuring communication, coordination and collaboration on a continuous basis up and down as well as across the organization. People who are energized.

The above requires a culture which focuses on values and beliefs which are consistent with allowing these characteristics to flourish. Leadership must be a role model – leading by example – their behaviors and practices always consistent with viewing people as their most important asset – investing in them from both a time and financial perspective. You must also have a purpose and a vision which excites people – which makes them willing participants and followers, committed to giving their best day in and day out.

It is unfortunate that studies conducted indicate that despite the money spent on leadership development every year, the quality of leadership around the globe has not improved. Other studies conducted by McKinsey have shown that it is not unusual for at least 40-50% of the people in an organization to feel disengaged because leadership abdicates or delegates one of their primary functions of engaging their people to others. Not only that, but much of what is taught in MBA/EMBA programs as well as executive development programs has been shown in similar research to be disconnected from the true business needs of an organization. Furthermore, as Gary Hamel cites in his book, "What Matters Now?", some of the management concepts still being utilized by organizations today are based upon approaches developed by Frederick Taylor and others nearly 100 years ago.

Allow me to share a simple example. I had the opportunity to work with the CEO and leadership team of the credit card operation of a large bank in the Balkan Region (e.g., Croatia, Serbia and others) for over a year. This particular operation, despite challenges offered to it by the parent bank and the recessionary business environment in the Balkans, this group had proven themselves to be one of the most successful American Express partners anywhere in the world.

In working with the leadership team, conducting regular strategic briefings on topics of value to help them be more successful, I was impressed in many ways. In particular, I told the CEO and the rest of the team that in my opinion they, as a leadership team, would rank in the top quartile or top 25% of all leadership teams I had worked with anywhere in the world. They were all very bright, capable/talented and motivated people.

However, what came through after many months was the fact that their staff – lower level employees had not been engaged. In fact, what could be said at best was that employees were being offered a job – and opportunity to come in each day, work and then collect a paycheck at the end of the month. An opportunity was being missed. We discussed it. I gave them homework to go out and talk with their employees which they did even though they seemed uncomfortable about doing it.

So the fact remains that it does not really matter how bright, capable/talented or turned on the leadership team is if they do not realize the importance of employee engagement or how to do it – namely if it remains a blind spot. Unless this is overcome the organization as a whole will never be able to achieve human performance excellence and therefore never be able, in my opinion, to reach its full potential for success.

Look at Tata, Nordstrom's, Google, Kimberly Clark and Gortex as just a few examples where the HPE characteristics mentioned above are alive and well.

AGILITY AND RESILIENCY

How should *agility* be properly defined? Have a look at the following definition which I use in my discussions with the leadership teams of organizations:

> *Agility is the capability of an organization to identify, assess and act on an opportunity (or threat) better and faster than the competitors.*

Look at Samsung versus Nokia, Blackberry versus Apple. Both of these situations provide an excellent example of one organization being more agile than their competitor.

What about resiliency? Here is how I would define it:

> *The capability of an organization to assess and take the most appropriate action with proper sense of urgency to address problem situations better and faster than any of their competitors would and, thus, minimize variation in performance and resume normal and stable performance at hyper-speed.*

Take J& J and their Tylenol situation many years ago. During the fall of 1982, for reasons not known, a malevolent person or persons, presumably unknown, replaced Tylenol Extra-Strength capsules with cyanide-laced capsules, resealed the packages, and deposited them on the shelves of at least a half-dozen or so pharmacies, and food stores in the Chicago area. The poison capsules were purchased, and seven unsuspecting people died a horrible death. Due to the quick, effective actions taken by J&J they were able to stem the problem quickly and completely without any further loss of life. Their response to this catastrophic event has been held as an exemplar for other to follow. Their sales returned to their normal levels almost immediately. This situation is in far contrast to the Firestone 500 Tire fiasco of the late 1970's or the more recent Lexus 'sticky gas pedal problem'.

One of the critical success factors associated with either agility or resiliency is having an exceptional sensing system as discussed in Chapter Five. Without it, your organization – your leadership team will be inhibited from making not only an optimal decision but being prevented from making it at hyper-speed if needed – instead they will be metaphorically *flying blind* or acting like *blind squirrels searching for nuts*. Sure, it is fast and easy to engage in knee jerk reactions, but 80% of the time, it will not be optimal – in fact, far from it. It will almost always and invariably be sub-optimal. You should be hoping that in your organization decision making is at least a zero-sum game. But in today's world, you need to be much better than that to grow and prosper.

Certainly there are cultural aspects involved – for as was discussed in Chapter One, culture can be the biggest inhibitor or enabler of organizational performance. As was discussed in Chapter Five, culture is one of the eight factors which most influences the speed and quality of decision making in an organization. And, besides, you need switched on (energized, motivated, passionate) people – not people who are asleep at the switch! Ensuring systematic approaches is also a key to success such as making certain you and your people are following the Deming plan, do/execute, measure and improve cycle as a part of daily work life.

RENEWAL

The concept of *renewal* is a relatively new one. It is what I believe can make a huge difference in the long-term stability of an organization's performance as well as its capability to create and deliver value and achieve unparalleled competitiveness and profitable growth. The following is an apt description: "the seamless and continuous integration of innovation, adaptation and learning". A tall order? Yes, but worth the effort.

Organizations should, after all, be a learning system – knowledge is being created, shared and refined on a continuous basis resulting in lessons learned – building a capability of being faster and better over time. It is a leadership team that consistently asks itself, "What can we do better or differently tomorrow to make this organization more successful long-term?"

It is this renewal concept that can keep your organization forever young. Renewal will prevent your business model from ever passing it's buy/sell date as this characteristic ensures continuous refreshing, re-energizing, re-thinking of what has been done and how it has been done to ensure the future is better than the past. Organizations such as Proctor & Gamble, Merck, and Nestlé which have been around a hundred years or more are not the same organizations they were when they started. They have undergone possibly five, ten, or 25 major changes over that time – an evolutionary process or metamorphosis. What does remain invariant is the purpose and certain of the values/beliefs and principles of engagement. So approach change on a smooth and continuous basis, not a jerky, one-off basis.

Some Notes on Innovation

Every organization needs to innovate to a greater or lesser extent depending upon its market positioning, product/service/support and technology. While innovation is not a silver bullet, it does remain one of many critical success factors – one of those vital few organizational competencies that will ultimately determine if your organization ever reaches its full potential.

The words "innovate or die" uttered many years ago by Tom Peters many years ago still apply. Why? Because innovation should be defined as follows:

Always looking for new or better ways of doing everything you do as an organization, which results in value being added to some stakeholder group.

That stakeholder group may be your employees, your customers, your suppliers, the local communities in which you have presence or society at large.

In my seminar entitled "Why efficiency is not a dirty word", I focused the discussion, at least in part, on how cycle time can result in generating the best out-of-the-box thinking – encouraging creativity and therefore innovation. In fact, it was shown how value can be driven by making your organization easy to do business with and being more responsive to stakeholders – not wasting their time or yours, keeping the emotional cost of doing business to a minimum and, in the process, reducing your own cost of doing business as well as that of your stakeholders.

In fact, I can tell you that when encountering executives from Motorola around the world, I have asked them, "If you had to do it again, would you still focus on improving quality reaching six-sigma levels?" The answer I got back was "no". I was told that if they had to it over, the focus would be on cycle time for reasons we have already discussed throughout this book including the above paragraph. I was told the same from Milliken and Xerox, two or the longest term leaders in quality.

However, it must also be said that to maximize the benefits or the value created and/or delivered through innovation, your people need to be willing to take the initiative, be creative and have passion – the essence of Human Performance Excellence and this, in turn, must be linked back to the culture of the organization. You see, it is all connected!

Furthermore, the full potential of your efforts will not be realized through incremental approaches. Why? Take a simple example. Suppose your current complaint management process results in a customer complaint be resolved in an average of 30 days. To get a 10% incremental improvement, you really do not need to change the process – you can pretty much keep doing what you've always done. However, if you wanted to reduce the average time to ten days, you would have to do things in a dramatically different way – re-engineer the process. Too often organizations just keep doing what they have always done, the way they have always done it, but expecting a different result. Einstein called this insanity! The fact of the matter, as Tom Peters in his 1987 book entitled, "Thriving on Chaos" puts it, "Incrementalism is the biggest enemy of innovation!"

However, even if you have empowered your people to take the initiative without fear, gotten their creative juices to flow and they have become passionate about what they are doing and why as well as having a supportive culture with the leadership team leading by example, the reality of innovation is that a lot of it will be little stuff albeit meaningful stuff. Here, have a look at the diagram below which depicts what this author has observed in his experience, right or wrong:

The Innovation Continuum

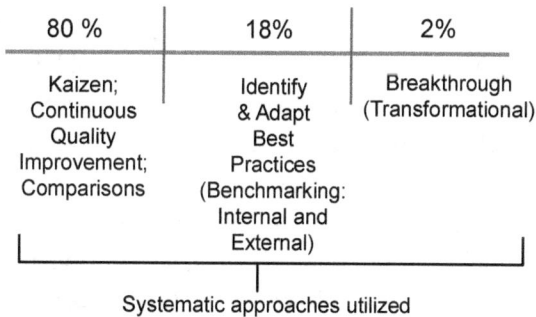

80 %	18%	2%
Kaizen; Continuous Quality Improvement; Comparisons	Identify & Adapt Best Practices (Benchmarking: Internal and External)	Breakthrough (Transformational)

Systematic approaches utilized

So it may be that even the best innovators like Apple and their iPad (breakthrough), 3M and their Post-It Notes (breakthrough) certainly have had their moments, overall, the vast majority of their efforts, probably close to 98% of them are far less dramatic. Certainly they are still engaged in doing those things which result in creating or adding value to some stakeholder group, but these would not be found in the headlines of U.S. News and World

Report or the Wall Street Journal. It does not, however, diminish their importance. It also says that to create a culture which supports the breakthroughs, you will generate 100 times as many smaller improvements of value.

A lot of it, certainly the 18% in the middle above, represent vital learning activity as does the first 80% where well documented systematic approaches to improvement and lessons learned sessions after each add to the knowledge base of the organization so it can be better and faster the next time – and every time after.

What to measure? Well there are many things one could consider. Again, no discussion of specific performance measurements or KPIs here, but have a look at the diagram below of a systematic process for innovation – it's what your process at the highest level should look like. Key performance measures can be determined using this diagram as a base. In the next volume, we will go into more specifics in terms of KPIs around innovation.

In the diagram on the facing page at least four issues deserve further mention. First is that your organization's innovation strategy, if it has one (hopefully it does), should link to your organization's overall competitiveness and growth strategy. In effect, innovation should be a driver of competitiveness and growth. Second, leadership must be educated – fully capable of supporting innovation throughout their organization. Third, every innovation should create value. Fourth, innovation needs to be integrated into your organization's cultural fabric and human performance excellence approach. Doing these four things will enhance the benefits derived from pursuit of innovation.

An overall management system for innovation and learning

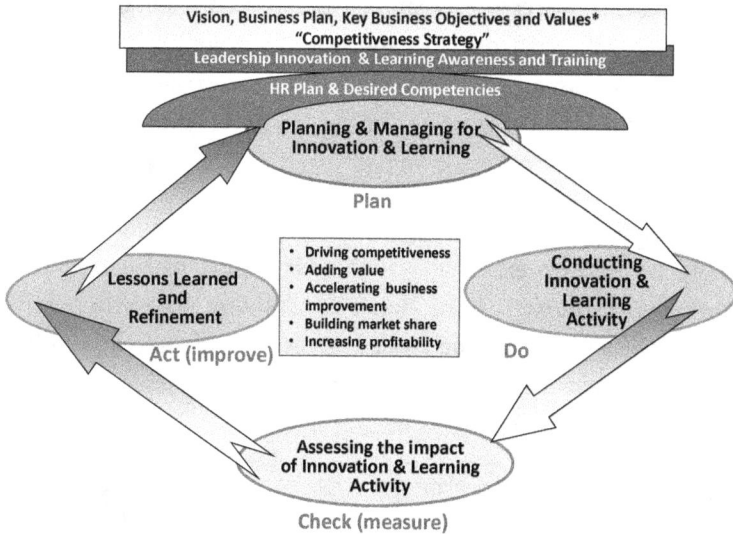

Vision, Business Plan, Key Business Objectives and Values*
"Competitiveness Strategy"
Leadership Innovation & Learning Awareness and Training
HR Plan & Desired Competencies

Planning & Managing for
Innovation & Learning

Plan

- Driving competitiveness
- Adding value
- Accelerating business improvement
- Building market share
- Increasing profitability

Lessons Learned
and
Refinement

Conducting
Innovation &
Learning
Activity

Act (improve)

Do

Assessing the impact
of Innovation & Learning
Activity

Check (measure)

* Innovation and Learning should be an organizational value AND must be woven into the fabric of your organization's culture. Linkages to Critical Success Factors and ALL appropriate HR Management Systems are also required.

So, what about adaptation?

First you have to ask, "Adaptation to what?" Well *change* of course! Change is all around us. Our markets, our customers, competition, technology, economic and social systems are changing continuously. You operate in a dynamic, turbulent environment where the only constant is change. However, unlike the dinosaurs who could not adapt to their changing environment and thus became extinct, you really don't want to go down that same path, do you?

It is also an environment in which you must be increasingly proactive – anticipating not only the changes, but their potential magnitude, direction and consequences for your organization. What are the alternate futures open to you? Where does your organization need to be in 18 months, three years, five years if you are to remain successful – competitive and maintain profitable growth?

Have a look at the chart below and ask yourself, "Where do you need to be tomorrow? What are the forces that are at work influencing what you must do and how you must do it to ensure your competitiveness and continued profitable growth tomorrow? How do you find out? What is the optimal path forward – the optimal positioning?"

Innovation tends to be a very internally driven and systematic approach, utilizing external stakeholder inputs as well as those from your people. This then results in positive external stakeholder impact through value addition. Adaptation tends to be a very externally driven and systematic approach with significant internal organizational impacts.

Innovation/New Opportunity Matrix

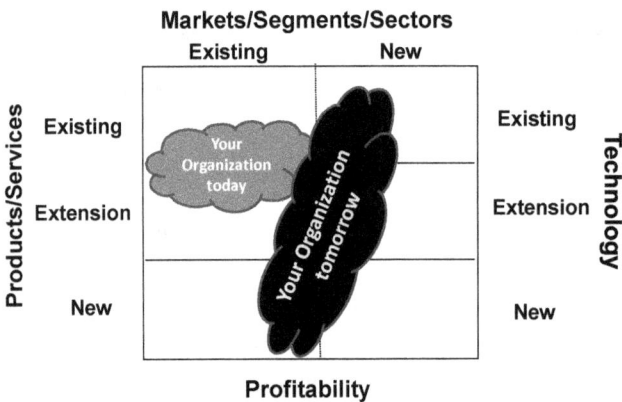

Agility: Capability to identify, assess and act on market opportunities better and faster than competition. Setting Priorities: market attractiveness including potential size of market (number of existing and "target" customers who have an interest and their potential profitability)

In addition, while agility is the continual one-off market focus on identifying, assessing and acting on an opportunity (and requires that sensing system we have discussed in order to be successful), adaptation has a holistic or total organizational focus. Have a look at the diagram on the facing page:

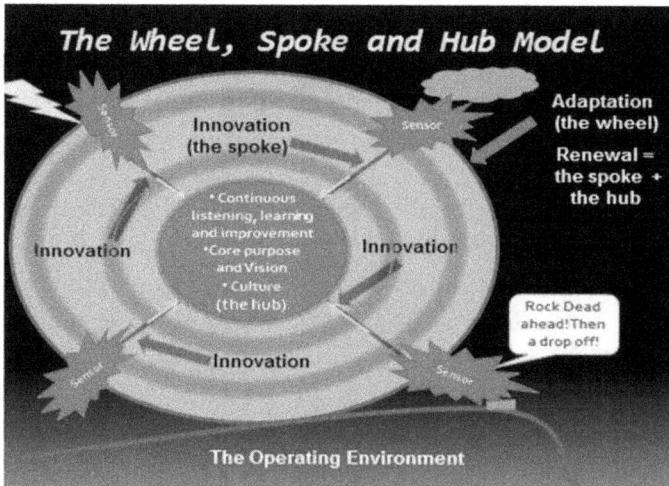

The Wheel, Spoke and Hub Model

Innovation (the spoke)

Adaptation (the wheel)

Renewal = the spoke + the hub

• Continuous listening, learning and improvement
• Core purpose and Vision
• Culture (the hub)

Innovation

Innovation

Sensor

Rock Dead ahead! Then a drop off!

Innovation

The Operating Environment

Through your organization's sensors (part of your sensing system) you are able to identify external changes or trends that are developing – to identify or even anticipate them and communicate these to the people who need to know them and act on them internally within your organization. At the same time people within your organization should be taking initiative, be empowered, passionate and creative – finding new and better ways to do things – to innovate and add value. How well this works depends largely on the culture which you and the leadership team have crafted. It also depends on how well your organization including the leadership team listens and learns from the data and information coming in through the sensing system. These two processes (innovation and adaptation) and the learning which takes place within each of them forms what I refer to as the renewal process of an organization. This was discussed also in Chapter One when we defined the Business Model of an organization.

So, how do you know if you are adapting? How well do you identify the extent to which you need to adapt? How do you avoid turning the need for change (adaptation) into a crisis because you waited too long – your sensors were dysfunctional or you were discounting or ignoring the inputs? How often have you had to adapt and to what? When was the last time and how well did you do and how well in advance did you detect the need for change? The hope is that you are answering these questions easily and in a way that clearly positions you and your organization as a role model for others to follow.

Just to conclude, you see that in all the above, learning is integral to all that your organization should be doing – your base of knowledge should be continuously refreshed or updated and your capability to innovate, to adapt should become faster and better as you move through time toward your destination – your vision!

There is little question that without a futures orientation, your organization will be at somewhat of a disadvantage. Every Management Committee meeting should contain an agenda item related to this topic. "What do we see coming – new emerging trends, changing requirements or operating conditions, technologies and so on." Always asking, "What have we done here today that will make us better tomorrow and how do we know? Are we securing our future or jeopardizing it by the decisions we have made here today?"

SOCIETAL BENEFITS

As was discussed in the previous chapter, the European Foundation for Quality Management Business Excellence Award first launched in 1992 contained a category focused on societal outcomes. It was ahead of its time. As you are probably well aware the focus on this issue continues to become an increasingly important one to people around the globe including your key stakeholders. It also is growing in its influence on your image/reputation as an organization and as a leadership team. It cannot be ignored without negative consequences to your organization.

In a recent Click TV Documentary on sustainable energy, the organizations with the largest data centers (Microsoft, Facebook, Google, Yahoo and Apple) use enough electricity to be the equivalent of the 6th largest country in the world! Of these,

Apple's data center uses 100% solar energy and 54% of Yahoo's comes from hydro-power. Again, this tends to have a rub off effect on these organization's image and brand strength. Organizations such as Johnson and Johnson, for example, who have their *principles of engagement* defined and operating well in such as areas as sustainability, ethical behavior, governance, corporate social responsibility and others, are held in higher esteem, often considered as one of the most admired organizations. Below is an excerpt from the most recent *J&J Citizenship and Sustainability Report.*

"Our commitment to citizenship and sustainability at Johnson & Johnson is inspired by what was written more than 70 years ago in Our Credo. To this day Our Credo serves as the compass that guides all decisions at our Company. Our Credo defines our responsibilities to all stakeholders and to the communities in which we work and live."

CEO & Chairman Alex Gorsky

The Company's Citizenship & Sustainability priorities are to advance human health and well-being, help to safeguard the planet, and lead a dynamic and growing business responsibly. This is the framework through which the Company strives to continue its progress on its current set of Citizenship & Sustainability five-year goals, which include:

- Advancing global health through research and development for neglected diseases and creating affordable access to medicines
- Building on the Company's legacy in helping to safeguard the planet by reducing the environmental impacts of operations and products
- Partnering with suppliers that embrace sustainability
- Fostering the most engaged, health-conscious and safe employees in the world
- Advancing community wellness
- Enhancing outcome measurement in philanthropy
- Committing to enhanced transparency and accessing the power of external collaboration

Health care is one of the greatest challenges facing society now and in the future. No other issue is as important or personal to every individual, every family, every community and every country. As the world's largest and most diverse health care company, Johnson & Johnson has a responsibility to lead in the development of a comprehensive and collaborative global approach to this challenge, and to continue pursuing our aspiration to help billions of people around the world live longer, healthier and happier lives.

One can create any number of relevant KPIs from this particular area of emphasis. While the full report of J&J will provide some further examples, it would be expected that your organization would have its own unique measures. For the full report have a look at the link: http://www.jnj.com/sites/default/files/pdf/cs/2013-JNJ-Citizenship-Sustainability-Report-FINAL061914.pdf.

EXECUTION

Some pretty frightening statistics are available in studies by the Economist, the American Management Association and others regarding strategy formulation versus strategy execution. For example, as reported by John Childress in his book, "Fastbreak", a recent survey of 200 FTSE (Financial Times Stock Exchange) 1000 companies revealed that 80% of directors said they had the right strategy, but only 14% thought they were implementing it well. If there is one area in want of improvement, it has to be the way organizations approach execution. Time and time again in organizations such as Siemens, Duke Power, Data General and so many others, I have observed a clear failure to execute effectively – not identifying the critical success factors or the potential barriers and how to obviate them effectively and efficiently. The world's greatest strategy poorly executed is worth nothing.

While Jack Welch has been somewhat discredited more recently regarding his specific strategies, the GE Leadership Center and his emphasis on building the capability of leadership throughout the organization has been a role model. Most recently GE is opening a satellite center in Indonesia to help three of its key clients there. What Jack has said about strategy execution below is instructive:

> Most strategies fail! Not due to lack of money or poor strategy, but a lack of good execution. The key isn't having a strategy, it's getting it implemented!

That pretty much says it all. So what is your strategy execution process? Do you have one? Is it working?

TECHNOLOGY, INFORMATION ARCHITECTURE AND NETWORKING

Technology

Ensuring your organization has a technology roadmap that goes out 18 months, three years and then beyond is a key. How obsolescence is identified and dealt with is another. Education of customers and other key stakeholders must be integrated into any discussions on this topic as well. Technology is obviously linked closely to innovation especially in high tech organizations such as Apple, Google, Samsung and many more. Utilizing the matrix shown above in this Chapter called the **Innovation/New Opportunity Matrix** may be a good place to start.

But once again, technology should not be developed in a vacuum. The approach of General Motors that "we are the experts and we know what the market wants" is long dead. The advent of customer labs at IBM and other organizations has been alive and well for years but needs to be extended to include other stakeholder groups – most notably your own people (especially frontline) and suppliers.

I still remember being asked to attend an emergency meeting of a Regional Telecom Company In Chicago after the decentralization of AT&T. The CEO and Management Committee informed me that they were in a panic. They had introduced two new services and one new product in the past six to nine months and all had failed miserably. I simply asked one question: "Did you talk to your customers first – involve them in the design or development of this product or these services?" The answer? No. Is there any wonder then that success was elusive?

However, at the same time, organizations *must* learn to respect the need for balance between *high tech* and *high touch*. Just how far can you go as an organization without losing touch or depersonalizing or sterilizing the relationships you have with your most important strategic stakeholder groups? This issue was discussed in Chapters Three and Four on value creation and delivery. Now, of course, digitalization is a topic of great interest to organizations. Again, I simply raise a caution. Namely, even a good thing carried to excess can be harmful.

Not all technology adds value and that still remains a key theme. It is also true that every organization should have goals set for achieving a certain percentage of its new products, services or support revenue representing next generation technology – continuous evolution, innovation and, where possible, a breakthrough that enhances the *quality of life* for those who must purchase and utilize your organization's products, services and/or support. Possibly you can create a *game changer* in your organization – something which changes the rules or basis of competition in your industry or sector.

Compaq Computer in Houston, Texas had a new product development and launch geared to a quarterly cycle. When I worked with them, one of the issues they experienced was that the problems which customers were having in Quarter 1 were not being captured or addressed fast enough and so these same problems were often being designed into Quarter 2 products, and on it went. No one was taking time to listen to the customer let alone act on their feedback. In the end, Compaq fell out of favor and was bought by HP.

The point here is that basic user problems or flaws in the product can eliminate any value that might be added in terms of new technology because current customers and potential customers become turned off about the product and wouldn't buy it regardless of what technology was incorporated into it. Certainly in any high tech industry, where the half-life of a product is getting shorter every day – that is, obsolescence is accelerated along with the acceleration in technology, there are risks if speed and efficiency are not embedded in the thinking and actions of your people from top management to frontline.

Information Architecture

Chapter Five was replete on the topic of sensing systems or Strategic Enterprise Information Architectures, so no need to go into more detail here. Again, any number of KPIs can be derived from the discussions contained in Chapter Five. But the fact remains that your sensing system is a critical success factor for your organization. Without one or the right one, you cannot achieve agility, you cannot be proactive, you will be unable to make optimal decisions better and faster – or at all.

The Sony Information Center was referenced earlier and it was indicated that once a year product development and those responsible for the user manuals/technical support would spend time talking with information center agents finding out the types of problems customers were experiencing either with products or the manuals. My point is, why wait a year to do this? You would agree that a lot can go wrong in a year – a lot that can cause permanent damage. Why not quarterly sessions? In the end the extra effort could have saved Sony many millions of dollars in warranty or service expense and loss in customer loyalty – a huge cost of lost opportunity as customers who once bought Sony moved to Samsung or other competitors.

For example, suppose that you had a global organization – spread out over 80 countries with 60 divisions and 100,000 employees. How do you approach employee satisfaction today? What methodology do you utilize and how do you compare results, separate holistic from local issues and set priorities? Suppose now that you could, on a quarterly basis, select a random sample of 25% of your workforce across the world and simply ask them to anonymously answer the following question and submit by email: "What does it feel like to work in this organization?" Then you could use Gavaghi (sentiment analysis) which was discussed in Chapter Five and has the capability to analyze quickly any form of communication – written or verbal and identify the underlying feelings, attitudes and intentions of people. The analysis would be able to show quickly the issues, where they are, whether holistic or local. It would become a pulsing system – again part of your overall sensing system.

Networking

No one has to tell us we live in a networked world. Social networks have taken on a life of their own. As a society, we are at a point where we depend increasingly on these networks for maintaining relationships, finding the music we want, interacting with others having similar business interests and the list continues. For organizations these social networks should be integrated into part of their sensing system – a potentially growing part.

However, experience has taught us that there is a great need closer to home for this networking activity. In many organizations because of the traditional silo mentalities and far flung global business structures, it is increasingly challenging to share ideas, to share learning, to feel as though we are all one team. Here are few examples.

For many years 3M Corporation was heralded as the father of innovation best practice. In my work with them I can certainly attest to the fact that they got some important things right. On a monthly and quarterly basis they would have teleconferences linking the scientific community within 3M across all divisions around the world for the purposes of sharing ideas and solutions. It was powerful and it worked – not just in terms of driving innovation, but in helping to foster teamwork – that all one team feeling which is critical to success. It also allowed for early detection of emerging trends.

Often a trend could develop in America and then be carried to Europe and then Asia over a certain period of time, possibly one to three years. Knowing this allows an organization to be creating a state of readiness to address the new trend. This might involve educating the public, for example.

Yet at the same time that 3M represents a great example of what can be done, there is another, quite different situation that existed at Corning Corporation. There, it turns out, three of Corning's largest divisions had the same company, Philips Electronics, as their top key account around the world in dozens of countries. Yet, never once, were the Corning people engaged with Philips in these divisions networked to share what they knew and how to better leverage it. A huge missed opportunity. This issue I have found to be more the rule than the exception in many organizations.

In Croatia I had the pleasure of working with a growing SME whose performance has been stellar to the point of garnering McDonald's global IT management responsibility. With really only three departments: sales, software development and technical support, little time is spent sharing what is being learned about McDonalds around the globe in the Middle East, Europe, China and so on where contacts take place in large numbers daily. Another missed opportunity for networking?

So, how do you ensure connectivity in your organization? Who is connected to whom? What sharing is going on regularly? It can be simple. The Vice President of Replacement Tire Sales at Goodyear where I worked at one time used to have a conference call every Saturday morning with his five Regional Managers. Honda HQ senior executives in Japan would make a point of regularly contacting key dealership owners to ask them what they were hearing from customers – were customer pleased, for example, with the way the car muffled sounds and felt smooth even when going over railroad tracks? So, what are you doing, who are you doing it with, what are you learning and how are you putting that learning to use to be more proactive, improve organizational performance or prevent problem occurrence?

How are you utilizing your networks to provide new product and service launch rapid feedback information so running changes, if needed, can be made at hyper-speed before it's too late and damage is incurred? I remember a situation where I was working with a golf equipment manufacturer in America. They called me in because of the need to contain a problem and prevent any further collateral damage associated with their newly designed clubs. They had been experimenting with light weight high strength materials for shafts on clubs such as titanium, composites and more.

At one point they thought they had arrived – Eureka! Their market position was quite enviable. In fact they were the preferred choice of the golf pros at hundreds of the top golf clubs across America. All these golf pros were sent a free set of the new high technology clubs. Unfortunately when used, the shafts began to crack and break. By the time the company reacted, virtually every golf pro in the country had experienced the problem and had lost trust and confidence in the company's brand. Trying to recover from that catastrophic event was next to impossible. One has to wonder if part of the problem was a rush to launch or a command from senior management that the announced launch date would be met come *hell or high water*.

This, by the way, I witnessed on numerous occasions while working at General Motors as well. In 1983 the new General Motors C-Cars, the Cadillacs being one of them, had to be outfitted with a new front wheel drive design and new generation front wheel drive transmission made of lighter weight materials. However, during tests at the Milford proving ground, this transmission showed a continuous pattern of random failures – the worst possible kind. Yet, GM decided to the launch the car on time and absorb the warranty costs – which they did. What they did not realize was the *hit* that was taking place on customer loyalty/repurchase as well as trust and confidence in the brand because of the problems. This is the same type of thinking that also led to the warranty costs on the Chevrolet Camaro in 1987 reaching the $1 billion mark! Ouch!

The lesson learned? Get it right before you launch it even if you must delay – as has sometimes been the case with Apple or Microsoft. The consequences of not doing it right can be catastrophic. Ensure a flawless launch. And, of course, as mentioned above, it makes sense to have that new product launch early warning system set up just in case.

RELATIONSHIP MASTERY

Previous chapters have implied that leadership, to be effective, needs to possess relationship mastery. It has been stated that having exceptional relationships with all key stakeholders is critical to organizational success. You may also recall the discussion in Chapter Five of the four components of a relationship review process. This relationship review will provide very rigorous, comprehensive and actionable information to help your organization build exceptional relationships with key stakeholders. However, it should not be your only source of such information. You will still need to integrate a number of sets of feedback from account management, complaints, your contact centers, and the list goes on (see the AT&T "Listening Post Team" example in Chapter Five). All of these form a part of your organization's sensing system or Strategic Information Architecture as was discussed in Chapter Five.

The other part of this performance component is that to be truly successful, an inclusive approach to relationships rather than an exclusive approach needs to be taken. Look at the work done by The Center for Tomorrow's Company, a think tank in London, for example.

This relationship approach, of course, includes internal working relationships just as much as external ones. In fact, Margaret Wheatley in her book some years ago called "Leadership and the New Science" brought home the point that the old Newtonian machine model of management just doesn't work in business. Whereas with an engine one might be able to optimize each component resulting in an engine which, as a whole, is optimized and more efficient, the same thing does not apply to an organization.

That is to say that if every little black box on the organizational chart was to be optimized, the entire organization as whole would, in fact, become suboptimized as each department or function would pursue what was in their best interest – not in the best interest of the organization as a whole.

At one time both DuPont and Nortel were failing to satisfy their customers. Why? Because the internal working relationships between groups were often dysfunctional – lack of communication, coordination, collaboration. Instead the intent was domination in some cases – one or more divisions or business units trying to be the ad hoc boss or vying for the position.

If your organization wishes to be an ideal supplier to a key strategic account, what are the criteria? Over the years, in countries around the world and interviews with the customers of organizations such as IBM, Xerox, Nortel, DuPont, J&J and the list goes on, a pattern has emerged in terms of what customers of these companies consider the characteristics of an ideal supplier one with which they can have a long-lasting and secure relationship. The facing page contains these characteristics.

If your key account customers were to rate your organization on a 1-5 scale where 1=poor and 5=excellent, how would you score on these characteristics?

The ideal supplier

Characteristics	Rating
Always "easy to do business with" – simple, uncomplicated	
Viewed as an "innovative" supplier – known for creative solutions	
The decision-making is very fast	
People who are empowered to make decisions at all levels	
People are state-of-the-art in their knowledge of products and technologies	
Always has enough resources to service our account in the best way	
Always "proactive" in terms of communication and solutions	
Understands our business and what makes it unique, better than the others	
Works as a "team" internally and with us, their customer	
There are excellent working relationships with our company at ALL levels – CEO down (we are "aligned for doing business the best way by counterpart")	

VALUE CREATION AND DELIVERY

This topic was discussed at length in Chapters Three and Four, where it was said that this was the true purpose of an organization. Everything you do should add value – not deduct it. There were some nine sources of value identified. The issue becomes, as previously, which ones are you utilizing, how well are you utilizing them and how do you know? Do your key stakeholders recognize and appreciate the value you are delivering to them? What about internally in the key internal working relationships – internal customers and suppliers – is value being created and recognized as well?

Value is the essence of differentiation and competitive advantage – use it wisely as it can make *all* the difference. It is also, as mentioned previously, the critical ingredient for building and maintaining exceptional and secure relationships with your key stakeholders.

From Chapters Three and Four, you can identify many potential indicators of value. Just keep in mind that the stakeholder is the ultimate judge of whether you have created and delivered value – whether that stakeholder is internal or external.

From a customer perspective, as mentioned before, you know you have provided value if you have reduced the customer's cost of doing business with your organization – either economic cost or emotional cost. Find out where your stakeholders are experiencing the greatest pain in their relationship with your organization or where the greatest pain exists between departments, functions, divisions or business units within your organization and reduce or eliminate it! Don't just focus on the economics!

COMPETITIVENESS AND PROFITABLE GROWTH

It should be clear that the previous nine areas of performance just discussed are, in fact, dimensions of what determines your organization's competitiveness and future profitable growth. Your job as the leadership team is to balance them, orchestrate the organization's resources and build its capabilities in a way that reinforces or supports achievement of competitiveness and profitable growth.

The bottom line remains. How do you distinguish your organization in the markets in which you compete? How do you rise above the noise level to become recognized as the best – as the preferred and recommended organization with which to do business? What have you done to ensure you have built an army of followers – stakeholders, customers who want to do business with your organization more than any other competitor? How do you know if you have created a secure unshakable, unbreakable set of stakeholder relationships with your organization?

Clearly too, your profitability should focus not only on your products, services and support, but also on your customers – segments as well as key accounts and your sales management (which really should be relationship management). What is the average profitability of each of your top ten key accounts and how has it grown each year over the past three years – why has it grown or not? On average, what is the period of loyalty of your customers – is it growing or shrinking and why? On average, how many products or services does a customer have? What if you could double that figure? What would the implications mean and how would you do it? What is the average revenue and growth in profitability by account manager – across all their accounts? Which account managers are performing the best and why? Performing the worst and why? What can you learn or do differently if improvement is needed?

Just a quick example that might be helpful to you. When working with Motorola, I suggested that they share with me a list of the current top 25 accounts. Then I asked them for that same list as of three years previous. Guess what? The lists were quite different! Many of the accounts on the list three years ago were no longer there or had dropped below 25th place this year. I asked why this had happened. No one knew the answer. Well, I am sure some account manager somewhere knew the answer, but they weren't talking in order to save themselves!

I also remember a time at Motorola when there was a celebration because fourth quarter sales had increased 25% from the previous year. Being curious, I asked management if they knew how much of that 25% was from two sources: (1) current customers who were so happy with Motorola that they increased their purchases; or (2) new customers who began doing business with Motorola as a direct result of an existing customer giving a positive reference. They had no clue. In the both cases it would have been prudent for Motorola to send out notes of appreciation to existing customers and a welcoming note to the new ones. Just make sure the increase in sales is not the result of a decrease in prices!

Well, the above descriptions should help identify areas of opportunity for your organization. All of the above represent potential KPIs or measures of success for your organization. All of them contribute to your competitiveness and profitable growth. How much weight each one will have depends on your organization's positioning, operating environment, customers, suppliers, and so on. It will not be the same for any two organizations. However, it is with confidence that I can say that all of these should be an element of any organization's KPIs moving forward, thus, showing up on your radar screen! The importance rating of these performance categories as mentioned previously would be expected to change over time, so be vigilant and diligent!

A Note on the Non-traditional Sources of Revenue and Profit

If there is one thing which I have observed over the past years in terms of how organizations pursue increases in revenue and profitability, it is that they often overlook the obvious. What do I mean? The following research results help to clarify the significance of this point:

- On average in most organizations, a 1% increase in customer loyalty is worth about a 9% increase in profitability (see Fred Reichheld, Bain and Company, "The Loyalty Effect" or the HBR journal article by Fred entitled, "Zero Defects Comes to Service". You will also find numerous detailed research from a variety of organizations – product, service environments shown in the book by Heskett et al, HBR Press, "The Service-Profit Chain", 1996). Similarly, the research by Bain also indicates that a 10% increase in customer retention equates to a 30% increase in the value of a company. So, do you have in place a customer retention team, fully empowered?

- It is not unusual for contact centers to receive as many as 20-33% unnecessary requests for information calls. Why? Customers are often not informed properly as information is not always effectively communicated by sales personnel or through available marketing information. If you estimate the cost of a typical call which averages five minutes and your contact center is receiving 5000 calls per day, the numbers add up quickly in terms of unnecessary cost — which, if eliminated, goes right to the bottom line.

- Similarly for complaints. If you are receiving 5000 complaints per year and the cost of resolution (administrative plus any adjustments) is $250 per complaint, again the numbers add up quickly if you reduce or prevent 25% of them.

The diagram below attempts to capture what I have learned from my 40 years experience working in this area.

Revealing the non-traditional sources of financial success

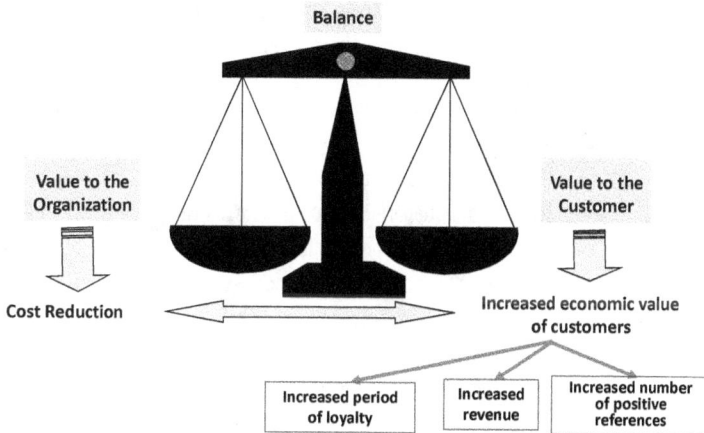

SUMMARY QUESTIONS FOR SENIOR MANAGEMENT BASED ON THIS CHAPTER

Answering the following questions should represent a learning opportunity for you and your MC members regarding Chapter Seven:

1. If you were categorizing your current KPIs (and drivers of those KPIs) into those which relate to Operational Excellence, what would you have?
   a. Does it provide you with a comprehensive view of what your organization is doing to pursue excellence in all aspects of your business:
      i. Process
      ii. Product

iii. Service
iv. Support
v. Technology
vi. Others?

b. What of the above information is used most frequently by each member of the leadership team? Why? What do they see as the benefit — the value in terms of insight which that measure brings?

c. Is there anything else each member of the leadership team would like to have — believes would allow them to be more effective or efficient as a senior manager?

d. Are there any gaps which you or your leadership team members believe exist — any areas where you really need more information to guide your decision making, priority setting, or resource allocations as you may have a blind spot now?

2. What is the quality program you have in place now and how effective is it? How do you know?

a. How do you ensure the highest quality (and fit for use) products, services and support on a continuous basis?

i. What is your process for monitoring and review of quality by the MC and setting of priorities for improvement and acting on them?

ii. How well have people throughout the organization been trained to build their capability and comfort level in the use of quality tools and techniques such as root cause analysis and prevention?

b. Does your program include lean six-sigma approaches?

i. Do you have any green-belts or yellow-belts?

ii. Do you have process ownership established to ensure continuous improvement and value creation and delivery?

c. What should be your number one priority for improvement for your organization's quality program?

i. How does each member of the MC feel about this issue?

ii. What best practice can you adapt and integrate into your approach?

iii. Do members of the leadership team teach some of the quality programs?

3. Have each member of the MC rate your organization on a scale of 1-5 where 1=poor, 2=fair, 3=good, 4=very good and 5=excellent in terms of how good a job is being done for your people:

a. Engaging them — increasing the emotional attachment they have to your organization so they feel good about working there, have a higher sense of commitment and look forward to coming in each morning.

b. Empowering them to do the right things for the organization and for the customer and other key stakeholders.

c. Motivating them so they are passionate about what they are doing and how they are doing it.

d. Ensuring they are taking initiative — that fear has been eliminated and if they make mistakes, they and the organization learns from it and goes on better than it was before.

e. Unlocking their creativity so that more out-of-the-box innovative approaches are integrated into your organization every day.

f. Having continuous, open and honest 2-way communication — ensuring transparency is the standard.

g. People are having fun, enjoying what they are doing and who they are doing it with and that gets communicated to all key stakeholders with which there is interaction on a daily basis.

h. People believe in excellence — being the best they can be and doing the best possible job first time, every time. The sense of pride is strong.

i. People feel that their learning curve is continually going up and that they are engaged in meaningful, value adding work — work that makes a difference — not just mundane, repetitive or routine activity.

Summarize the results for the leadership team and see where you can make significant improvements. Anything with an average score of 3 or less is fair game for improvement. Set action plans and establish ownership to get it done.

4. What does agility mean to you and your MC? How should it be defined for your organization so everyone *gets it*?

a. How would you rate the level of agility of your organization today on a scale of 1-5 where 1=poor, 2=fair, 3=good, 4=very good and 5=excellent?

b. What do you and the MC believe are the factors that can contribute most to making your organization more agile and why is it important to do so?

i. What is one positive strategic/competitive move your organization has made in the past 18-24 months that you and the MC would consider to be an excellent example of agility?

    ii.   What was the benefit to the organization? To your key stakeholder groups? To your organization's competitiveness?

    iii.   What was most difficult about making this happen? Why?

  c. What are the factors that are holding your organization back from being more agile today — possible barriers?

    i.   What are you and the MC going to do about them — to build your organization's capability?

    ii.   What are your priorities? Who will own those priorities? What are the first three steps you need to take?

    iii.   How will you measure your success in making your organization more agile — moving to a 5 on a 5-point scale? What will be the value of doing so for the organization and your key stakeholders?

5.   What does *resiliency* mean to you and your MC? How should it be defined for your organization so everyone *gets it*? Why is it important?

  a. How would you rate the level of resiliency of your organization today on a scale of 1-5 where 1=poor, 2=fair, 3=good, 4=very good and 5=excellent?

  b. What do you and the MC believe are the factors that can contribute most to making your organization more resilient and enduring, and why is it important to do so?

    i.   What is one positive strategic/competitive or operational move your organization has made in the past 18-24 months that you and the MC would consider to be an excellent example of resiliency?

    ii.   What was the benefit to the organization? To your key stakeholder groups? To your competitiveness?

    iii.   What was most difficult about making this happen? Why?

  c. What are the factors that are holding your organization back from being more resilient today — possible barriers?

    i.   What are you and the MC going to do about them — to build your organization's capability?

    ii.   What are your priorities? Who will own those priorities? How will you measure your success in making your organization more resilient — moving to a 5 on a 5-point scale?

    iii.   What will be the value of doing so for the organization and key stakeholders?

6. What does *innovation* mean to you and your MC? How should it be defined for your organization so everyone *gets it*? Why is it important?

    a. How would you rate the level of innovation of your organization today on a scale of 1-5 where 1=poor, 2=fair, 3=good, 4=very good and 5=excellent?

    b. Is it an organizational value/belief — part of the fabric of your culture?

    c. What should be your personal role in innovation?

    d. Do your HR systems such as recognition, performance appraisal and reward contain elements related to innovation to reinforce the behaviors, practices and results you need and want in this area of innovation?

    e. What do you and the MC believe are the factors that can contribute most to making your organization more innovative? What would your customers and suppliers say? How do you compare to competition?

        i. What would you and your MC agree upon has been the most recent (18-24 months) and best example(s) of innovation by your organization?

        ii. What was the benefit to the organization? To your key stakeholder groups? To your competitiveness?

        iii. How do you ensure that innovation is not just a one-off but a continuous process?

        iv. What should be the personal contribution of each member of the leadership team to innovation? What about their department/function/division/business unit?

    f. What are the factors that are holding your organization back from being more innovative today — possible barriers?

        i. What are you and the MC going to do about them — to build your organization's capability?

        ii. What are your priorities? Who will own those priorities?

        iii. How will you measure your success?

        iv. What will be the value of doing so for the organization and key stakeholders? To your organization's competitiveness?

7. What does *adaptability* mean to you and your MC? How should it be defined for your organization so everyone *gets it*? Why is it important for your organization to adapt continuously as opposed to taking a crisis approach? Do you have any examples of the latter?

a. How would you rate the level of adaptability of your organization today on a scale of 1-5 where 1=poor, 2=fair, 3=good, 4=very good and 5=excellent?

b. What do you and the MC believe are the factors that can contribute most to increasing your organization's level of adaptability?

   i. What is one positive strategic/competitive move your organization has made that you and the MC would consider to be an excellent example of your organization's adaptability to change in your operating environment recently e.g., past 24-36 months maximum?

   ii. What was the benefit to the organization? To your key stakeholder groups? To your competitiveness?

   iii. What was the most difficult aspect of the adaptation? What was your role as the leadership team?

c. What are the factors that are holding your organization back from being more adaptable today e.g., unable to let go of old paradigms, past approaches or technology platforms or others?

   i. What are you and the MC going to do about them — to build your organization's capability?

   ii. What are your priorities? Who will own those priorities?

   iii. How will you measure your success?

   iv. What will be the value of doing so for the organization and key stakeholders? To your organization's competitiveness?

8. If you and your MC were to summarize the most important *learnings* each has had as a result of working in the organization during the past 24 months, what would they be? Is there any consistency or does each member of the leadership team have different learnings?

a. How well have you and members of the leadership team learned and shared that learning? Do you have a process or method you use, e.g., a lessons learned activity on a regular basis after execution of plans/strategies or initiatives to determine what was learned, what could be done better or differently the next time or stepping back and reflecting on the consequences of actions taken whether resource allocations, competitive moves or others?

b. Is it important to you and the leadership team that learning is taking place at all levels across the organization? Why? What are the consequences of not learning on a continuous basis over time or throughout the organization?

    c.   On a scale of 1-5 where 1=poor, 2=fair, 3=good, 4=very good and 5=excellent, have each member of the leadership team rate the degree to which you could call your organization a learning organization i.e., learning is occurring at all levels and across the organization on a continuous or daily basis and that learning is driving the performance of the organization and its people in a positive direction.

        i.   What changes or improvements, in priority order, need to take place to get to a '5'? For example, what steps could be taken to accelerate learning within your organization?

        ii.   What would be the benefits (the value) of doing so for the organization and all key stakeholders? For its competitiveness?

        iii.   What will be most difficult and why? How will you address it?

9.   Looking at the *innovation/new opportunity matrix* from earlier in this chapter, break the leadership team into groups of four to six members. Each group will have a flip chart to draw the following:

    a.   Where they believe the organization is today

    b.   Where they believe it needs to be in 18 months to three years

    c.   Each group will explain their output

    d.   Each group will explain how their future picture helps to

- add value to the organization and key stakeholders
- eliminate or reduce vulnerabilities
- leverage organizational and core competencies for increased competitive advantage
- contribute to greater profitable growth for the organization
- increase competitiveness.

10.   Discuss what the concept of *renewal* means to you and your leadership team.

    a.   Why should it be a strategically important concept to your organization? What are the benefits?

    b.   How do you believe the organization can do a better job of seamlessly integrating its innovation, adaptation (to change) and learning approaches to enhance its competitive position long-term?

        i.   Identify the first three steps that would need to be taken to achieve this integration.

        ii.   Identify two to three key measures of success that would tell you it was enhancing your organization's performance regarding renewal.

  iii. Where should the ownership be for making this happen?

  iv. What will be the most difficult aspect of getting it right?

11. How would you and the leadership team describe or summarize your organization's *principles of engagement* — those issues related to sustainability, governance, ethical business practices, corporate social responsibility or others *in a clear and concise statement* — one which employees, customers and suppliers as well as other stakeholder groups can easily understand? (See the J&J example provided in this chapter.)

 a. What are the specific outcomes which you and the leadership team are hoping to achieve? How will you know if you are making progress in achieving these outcomes?

  i. Are these outcomes consistent with the *expectations* of your key stakeholder groups including your employees and customers? How do you know?

  ii. How has your thinking and that of the leadership team evolved on this issue over the past two to three years?

  iii. What are you doing now that you were not doing three years ago? Why did you take action? What do you believe the benefit has been? Can it be measured? How?

  iv. What do you and the leadership team think you will be doing in these areas three years from now that will be different or better?

 b. How can you determine or assess the value that addressing these issues is having on your organization's image/reputation or strength of brand?

12. On a scale of 1-5 where 1=poor, 2=fair, 3=good, 4=very good and 5=excellent, how would you rate your organization in terms of its capability or success in *consistently and completely executing* plans, initiatives, strategies over the past three years?

 a. What do you and your leadership team members believe are the most important priorities for improvement that need to be made to move your organization's execution score closer to a '5'?

 b. What do you and the leadership team members believe are the top three reasons why execution has not been as good as it could or should have been? In your priorities for improvement above in 12a, will these three reasons be addressed?

 c. What process or methodology do you utilize now, if any, to better ensure plans, initiatives and strategies are executed as flawlessly and completely as possible to ensure their full intended impact?

i. Is it a systematic, integrated and comprehensive approach/process?

ii. Is ownership and accountability clear?

iii. Is empowerment given?

iv. How often do your monitor progress?

v. What if mid-course changes or corrections are needed during execution, how efficiently and effectively does that happen and who is involved?

vi. Does the capability exist in your people to get the job done? What else might be helpful to the cause — eliminating barriers to their performance (e.g., better communication or greater involvement in the formulation to improve buy-in), building their capabilities?

13. Is your organization viewed in the marketplace as being a leader in the development or use of technology — an innovator? How do you know?

a. How do you and your leadership team believe you have been most successful in integrating technology into your products, services and support in a way that your stakeholders perceive (see and experience) value being added which translates into clear benefits for them?

b. How do you and your leadership team believe you have been most successful in integrating technology into the organization for the benefit of your people — enabling them to be more effective, efficient and add more value in their internal working relationships as well as in those relationships with external customers and other key stakeholder groups?

c. What have been the most important information technology improvements or innovations you have integrated/adopted/adapted in your organization in the past three years and what has been the benefit of doing so in terms of overall organizational performance, people performance, stakeholder satisfaction, and competitiveness? How do you know?

14. How would you and the leadership team define *networking* for your organization?

a. If networking, to a large extent, involves ensuring connectedness of people across the organization to enhance their feeling of being all one team; allow for the more effective and efficient exchange of ideas and knowledge — whether market, customer, competitive, emerging trends, technology, changing requirements or other;

facilitate communication, coordination and collaboration; as well as ensuring linkages to external industry/technology experts or stakeholder groups, how would you rate your organization on a scale of 1-5 where 1=poor, 2=fair, 3=good, 4=very good and 5=excellent?

    i.   What do you and your leadership team see as the greatest opportunities to improve networking in your organization – to move it closer to a '5'? What would be the value of doing so?

    ii.   What are the greatest barriers to improving the networking in your organization? How do you overcome them?

    iii.   Have you and the leadership team members solicited employee input on this topic to understand their views and suggestions? How can you best involve your people in making any meaningful changes needed?

15.   How would you and your leadership team define *relationship mastery* for your organization?

    a.   Why is it important to the success of your organization? How can it help your organization achieve a sustainable competitive advantage?

    b.   What is the level of comfort and success you and each member of your leadership team would have if placed in conversations with senior executives of key stakeholder organizations including key accounts for the purpose of strengthening the business relationship? Use a scale of 1-5, where 1=poor, 2=fair, 3=good, 4=very good and 5=excellent.

        i.   What should be the most important priorities for improvement to move you and the members of the leadership team to a '5'?

        ii.   What needs to be done for the people in your organization below the leadership team level? What groups in particular should be a priority and why (e.g., frontline)? Who should be the owner or be held accountable for making this happen?

        iii.   In the conversations suggested above, what questions would you ask to strengthen the relationship? What issues would you focus attention on?

16.   Discuss the *Ideal Supplier* survey covered in this chapter, and the relevancy of the questions to your organization. Note that, in general, the issues contained in the questions of that survey could apply to

virtually any stakeholder relationship. Hold a session with your leadership team. Select either a key account or other key strategic stakeholder organization and complete the ideal supplier (or provider) survey. Have each member of the leadership team rate your organization on a scale of 1-5 where 1=poor, 2=fair, 3=good, 4=very good and 5=excellent.

    i.   What is the degree of agreement among the leadership team members? Discuss the differences and similarities – come to agreement on what reality looks like for your organization.

    ii.   What do you see as your organization's strengths?

    iii.   What should be your top priorities for improvement to move you closer to a '5'?

    iv.   Who should be involved in making these improvements and who should take ownership and be held accountable?

17.   How do you and your leadership team believe *value* should be defined in your organization?

    a.   In Chapters Three and Four the concept of value was discussed in detail and you and your leadership team members were asked a series of questions. In this section, your assignment is to answer the following:

        i.   Determine what your B2B and B2C customers would consider to be of value to them. What would add benefits in doing business with your organization that could strengthen the relationships further, making them secure customers? It is suggested that in-depth interviews and focus groups be conducted. Use the information contained in Chapters Three and Four as a basis for your questions in performing this qualitative research, especially the relationship review. It is also suggested that members of the leadership team be grouped in twos and asked to conduct the research, collecting the information and bringing it back to share with their colleagues at the next MC meeting.

        ii.   Do the same for your key suppliers.

        iii.   Do the same for your own organization's people.

    b.   What are your conclusions?

        i.   What actions should be taken?

        ii.   Who should be the owners – where should the accountability be?

18.   What do you and your leadership team members believe are your organization's current and true *competitive advantages*?

    a.   Have each member of the leadership team make their list of three to five, share and compare. Come to agreement.

    b.   Is it clear that those characteristics distinguish your organization from the rest of the pack or can help your organization rise above the noise level to stand out in some important way to the customer?

    c.   How many of them can provide a long-term advantage versus a shorter-term advantage? What can you do to better ensure your competitive advantages will be longer lasting?

    d.   Are these advantages sufficient for now? Sufficient in 18 months? Three years? What actions need to be taken to maintain competitive advantage as you move forward? What are you critical vulnerabilities (be open and honest — candor is critical as is constructive debate among leadership team members) and how do you address them? How soon do you need to address them? What actions need to be taken? Who should have ownership/accountability?

19.   What would be three to five priorities for action you and your leadership team members would suggest be taken as soon as possible to ensure significant profitable growth over the next 18 months to three years or beyond?

    a.   How would you define significant? Is there agreement?

    b.   Have each team member make their list

        i.   Each member will share their lists along with their rationale

       ii.   Discuss/debate

      iii.   Reach agreement

    c.   What contribution could each leadership team member or his/her organization make?

20.   How effectively do you use cycle time as a way to drive innovation? What other key sources of innovation do you utilize and what percentage comes from: your people, your customers, competitors, best-in-class or best practice examples or comparisons, your suppliers/supply or value chain partners, cycle time, R&D or crisis (the Mother of all invention!)? How successful have you been in avoiding an incremental approach to your business which has been shown to be the biggest enemy of innovation?

21.   In each of your Management Committee meetings do you ask the following questions as your last agenda items:

a.   What have we done here today — by our decisions, priorities, resource allocations that better secures our future success rather than jeopardizing it and how do we know?

b.   What tells us that we, the leadership team, are working together as all one team?

c.   Have we taken time to step back from our day-to-day firefighting and think strategically about the organization, its operating environment, new emerging trends, changing requirements of our stakeholders, the future of competition, where we need to be in 18 months or three years in terms of new products/services or extensions, technologies, markets and the consequences so we better ensure continued profitable growth?

d.   Have we been true to our purpose and vision by what we have done today?

22.   How effective is each member of the MC at building and maintaining exceptional working relationships with each key stakeholder group including your people. Are they willing and inspired followers? Has accountability for this been established? How effective has it been?

23.   Based upon everything you have read in this short book and looking at the new generation balanced scorecard suggested above and understanding in-depth your organization's context/culture and operating environment, vision, purpose, critical success factors and principles of engagement, what would you and each member of your leadership team assign as an importance weight out of 100% in answer to the following?

a.   The importance weight each member of the leadership team believes each of the nine performance categories has today for your organization.

b.   The importance weight each member of the leadership team believes each performance category will have in 18 months and then three years for your organization.

c.   Compare and discuss in each case above.

d.   What are your conclusions as a leadership team?

   i.   What should be your priorities for action and when?

   ii.   Who should have ownership/accountability?

I do hope I hear from you. If you find that pursuing the answers to the questions at the end of each chapter have, in fact, made a difference, I'd like to know of it. Share with me how it helped you and your organization to reach a better place: ted.marra@informeddecisions.se.

www.ingramcontent.com/pod-product-compliance
Lightning Source LLC
Chambersburg PA
CBHW052124230326
41598CB00080B/4319